The island of waters and dreams

ATHENS 2002

Text: Sophia Piskopani
Edited by: Daphne Christou
Translated by: Judy Giannakopoulou
Photography: Antonis Solaris, M. Toubis S.A. Archives
Design: Evi Damiri
Colour Separations, printing: Michalis Toubis Graphic Arts S.A.

Nisiza Karela, Koropi
Tel: (010)6029974, Fax: (010) 6646856
http://www.toubis.gr

ISBN: 960-540-440-0

Warm thanks to Mr V. Tselepidis (geologist) and Mr G. Sphikas (special research in the natural environment); also to Antonis Solaris for the photographs he made available to us, that proved particularly valuable in the publication of this tourist guide to Andros.

On your lips there is a taste of storm
But where have you wandered
All day long with the hard reverie of stone and sea
An eagle-bearing wind stripped the hills bare
Stripped your desire to the bone
And the pupils of your eyes seized the relay-rod of the Chimera
And lined memory with traceries of foam!

From "Marina of the Rocks"*

Poem by Odysseus Elytis, translated by Kimon Friar
from Odysseus Elytis: *The Sovereign Sun and Selected Poems*,
Bloodaye Books, Newcastle upon Tyne, 1990

CONTENTS

1. ANDROS

2. HISTORICAL INTRODUCTION

3. CULTURE & TRADITION

4. TOUR OF ANDROS

CONTENTS

Andros (Chora)

Gavrio

Batsi

Korthi Bay

5. TWO-DAY ESCAPE TO ANDROS

Liopesi.

1 ANDROS

·he island of waters and dreams

If you still believe in miracles, Andros is prepared to confirm your faith and reward you with memories that are appropriate only to miracles: beyond reason and any natural order. Combinations of blue and white, dry-wall masonry, windmills, light, fast sailing ships and dovecotes are among the images that will be imprinted on your memory and, for a moment, you may think you're on yet another Cycladic island. But you'll be wrong. Because Andros is that, and much more. It is, first of all, the island that adds new colours to the Cycladic palette. It is a feast of colours and sensations. It is also the island on which you lose count of the number of springs gushing forth crystal waters, and the countless beaches – heavily populated and organised as well as isolated and deserted – and you have a hard time deciding which one to visit first.

On Andros, everything exudes a feeling of old-world nobility and refined taste. This is the result of its inhabitants' long contact with the sea, which on the one hand brought the seamen's families some financial comfort, and on the other lent the island the aura of distant places. On the islands, you see, the winds of change blow frequently, from various directions, so that caution and prudence are required for change to be assimilated in a constructive and creative way. The inhabitants of Andros, or Andriots, know this lesson well, for they have ensured both that tradition is respected on their island and that they themselves remain genuinely cosmopolitan.

Zorkos.

Here, contemporary art galleries play host to the works of great painters, and sculptures carved by the hands of local artists adorn various corners of the island. The summer season is ideal for encounters with the visual arts, since on Andros one has the opportunity to become familiar with the work of some of the most significant artists in the world. Where better to host works of art than a place that even the most fleeting glance will confirm is as unique and timeless as every great creation?

On Andros one can admire the architecture, which, although generally Aegean, has some singular features of its own: its folk art that follows the dictates of the natural environment; its people and the narrow, picturesque streets; the peace and vigilance; the constant values and the restless commercial spirit that have anchored in some of the world's most important ports.

And then returned home.

As we, too, will return. Because so few such paradises remain on our planet that we wouldn't exchange them for anything.

Haven't people always been like that? Searching for something new, but always nostalgic for paradise?

Andros, aristocratic and spare, attracts people who yearn for paradise.

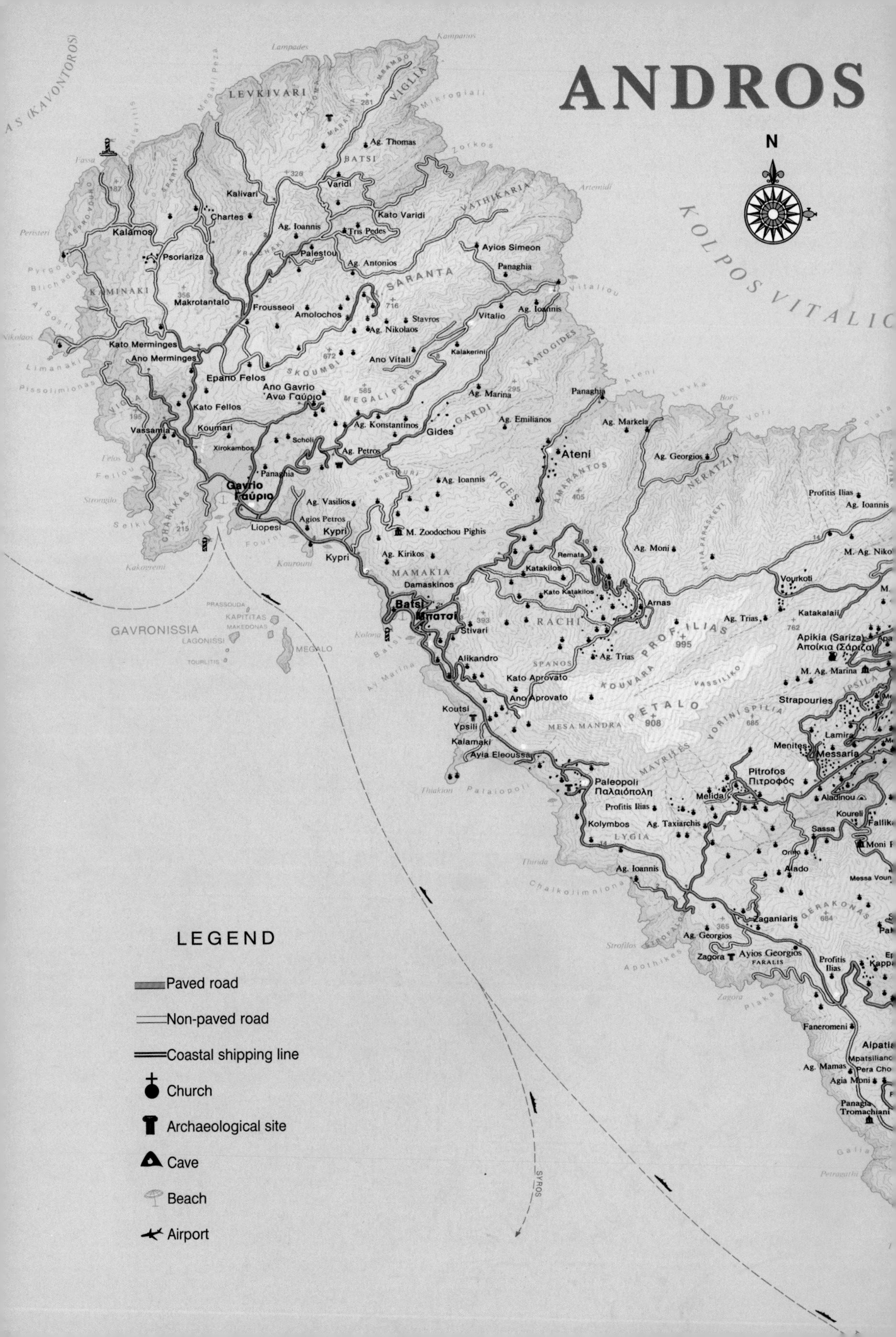

ANDROS
N
KOLPOS VITALIO
LEGEND
Paved road
Non-paved road
Coastal shipping line
Church
Archaeological site
Cave
Beach
Airport
Gavrio
Γαύριο
Batsi
Μπατσί
Paleopoli
Παλαιόπολη
Pitrofos
Πιτροφός
Ateni
Arnas
Messaria
GAVRONISSIA
SYROS

Geography

Location

Andros is the northernmost island of the Northern Cyclades with an area of 374 km^2, making it second only to Naxos in size. According to the 1991 census, it has approximately 8500 inhabitants. It is south of Evia, from which it is separated by the strait named Kafireas or Cavo d'Oro (7 miles wide), and north of Tinos. A narrow channel 0.8 miles wide called Steno (or Avlona) separates it from Tinos. The island is positioned along an axis from northwest to southeast. Its maximum length is 39 km. and maximum width is 16.7 km. The total length of its coastline is 177 km. It is generally a mountainous island, with lush ravines and valleys and abundant surface and ground waters.

Terrain

There are four mountainous sections of Andros, which are laid out in parallel at right angles to the vertical axis of the island. From north to south we find: a) Ayii Saranta, b) the Petalo-Kouvara massif that contains the island's highest peak, c) Gerakonas and d) Rachi. There are also four corresponding parts of the island between and around the mountains, which include hills and valleys: a) the hills of Makrotantalo (average height 200 m.), with the valleys of Felos and Gavrio, b) the region of Katakilo-Batsi, c) the valley of Mesaria and d) the valley of Korthi. In accordance with the recent change in the administrative division of the island, Andros consists of the municipalities of Andros, Hydrousa and Korthi. A characteristic feature of Andros is its abundant and high quality water. It is the richest of the Cycladic islands in terms of surface waters, with ravines and streams that contribute decisively to the landscape (vegetation, shaping of the coasts). The largest of these streams, with the most uninterrupted flow, is the Achla. The island also has many springs, the largest of which is the Zenio on Mt Petalo, at an altitude of 900 m., which flows into three different streams (Melida, Nimborio and Yialia). In the foothills of Petalo, there is also a famous spring at Apikia, the Sariza spring with medicinal properties.

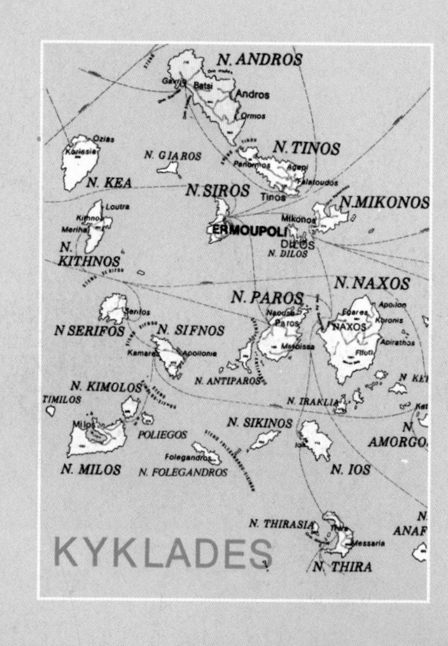

The **climate** of Andros is generally healthy and pleasant. Even in mountainous areas it is almost mild due to its proximity to the sea. After summer, the warmest season is autumn. But even in summer, the air temperature is relatively cool, owing to the meltemi winds blowing from the north more frequently between late July and early September. Because of the more general prevalence of north winds, there is a large concentration of water vapour on the northern slopes of the mountain massifs, with the result that some villages (Amolochos, Arni, Vourkoti, Katakalaii) are almost permanently overcast. The regions at a middle altitude, especially the leeward ones, have comparatively low humidity. The north winds are less strong in the western part of the island (Gavrio to Steno), where higher temperatures are recorded than in the east. Rainfall on Andros is the highest in the Cyclades for all months, double even that of Athens in the winter. In summer there is little rain. Snow is not rare, especially in the mountains, and more likely in January and February. On the contrary, hail and storms are rare.

1

1. The cave of Aladino
2. The rocky region of Vori
3. Vestiges of the mine at Ayios Petros.

2

Geology

Geotectonically, Andros belongs to the Attic-Cycladic mass and consists of two tectonic entities: an upper one, called the Makrotantalo entity, dating to the Upper Paleozoic era (i.e. more than 250 million years old) and the lower, central-south entity of unknown age.

The contact between these two entities is tectonic and has been identified in a composite zone with overlying rocks (igneous, magmatic) that have been warped similarly to the warped rocks of both entities.

The Makrotantalo entity, which is limited in area to the north-western part of the island, from the Kampanos cape to the Kakogremi cape, consists of schists such as amphibolites, micaceous schists and marble, within which tiny fossils have been found which testify to a Permian age (between approximately 285 to 245 million years). The lower entity, which occupies all the rest of the island, consists of marble alternating with various types of schists.

The entire range includes metamorphosed rocks in which fossils have not been found, and therefore these rocks cannot be dated. Scattered over a very small area there are appearances of rocks generated by explosions, as well as acidic veins (region north and west of Fellos in the western part of the island and in the Kremides region), granite-diorite in the Barada area (north-west of Kato Katakilo) and serpentinites as serpentine peridotites over a large area of the northwestern section (scattered throughout the Epano Fellos region to the south-west up to the Mikroyali Bay in the northeast, as well as from the coast of Platanisto Bay to Vori Cape in the northeast). The more recent rocks on Andros, carbonate sandstones with macro-micro fossils, can be encountered on isolated sites mainly in the coastal regions of the island.

The lateral findings, consisting mainly of loose breccias and blocks with frequent and large appearances in the central part of the island, are regarded as being among the fairly modern depositions as are the alluvial silts of streams and gullies consisting of sand, clays and shingles.

Andros is rich in minerals. Ayii Saranta in particular and the surrounding hills are rich in iron and manganese ores, copper and less frequently lead and zinc.

Andros is also known for its mineral springs. Some of them well up through tectonic fissures. The best known of them are on Petalo (Paleopoli, Vourkoti, Menites (Zanaki spring) and two in Apikia (Sariza and Ayia Irini, etc.).

3

Flora and Fauna

Andros is the Cycladic island with the richest flora which, because of the lack of homogeneity throughout, offers the visitor a variety of impressions. Greenery is abundant especially on the eastern side of the island, which receives most rainfall and where the mouths of most of its streams are located (from north to south: Arnipotamos, Achla, Yialia, Louria, Alado or Livadia, Dipotamata etc.). At the higher altitudes, the plant covering is poor, owing to the strong winds. In some places, however, there are self-sown forest trees (oak, walnut, etc.). The richest vegetation at high altitudes can be found on Petalo. At the middle and lower altitudes, shrubs are found in abundance (mastic, arbutus, linden, wild olive trees, etc.). At damper points one can find myrtle, broom, laurel, oleanders and others. In the deepest parts of the valleys there are clumps of plane trees, poplars, weeping willows, reeds etc. There are a great many olive, mulberry, apple, almond and fig trees. Another characteristic feature of the Andriot landscape is the presence of cypress trees, mainly near settlements or cultivated areas.

Andros, as well as all of the rest of Greece, could be called a botanist's paradise. It has been estimated that throughout Greece as a whole, many species of plants thrive. On the Aegean islands (not including Crete) there are at least 80 species of indigenous Greek flora. Andros is rich in plant life, and in springtime it is a riot of wild flowers such as anemones, poppies, orchids, irises and bellflowers.

On the island of Andros there are also rare endemic plants. Some of them are: Silene pentelica, Hypericum delphicum, Galanthus ikariae subsp. snogerupii and Campanula sartorii which grows on Mt Petalo.

Andros has the richest and most interesting vegetation in the Cyclades.

The Aegean islands play an important part in ornithological life.

Birds migrating to and from Africa and Northern Europe use the islands as a resting place on their long journey.

On Andros in particular, rare species of birds of prey nest, such as the kestrel, peregrine falcon, Eleonora's falcon and Bonelli's eagle. Within the low vegetation, the chukar partridge finds refuge. On the island's rocky coasts nests the feral rock dove (columba livia), while near settlements one finds the collared turtle dove.

In addition, one can find night birds of prey such as the owl or even the blackbird or rock thrushes, which build their nests on the island's rocky coasts, and the wren.

Birds like the blue tit (Parus caeruleus) and great tit (Parus major) also seek a place of refuge to nest on the island, as does the finch, goldfinch, linnet, swallow, house martin, red-rumped swallow, nightingale and lark. And finally, in migration season, many other birds cross the island's skies including bee-eaters, hoopoes, cuckoos, glossy ibis, herons, terns and many species of sparrows.

HISTORICAL INTRODUCTION

Pre-history

We find references to Andros in the writings of several authors in antiquity (Strabo, Herodotus, Thucydides, Pausanias, Stephanus Byzantinus, Diodorus Siculus, etc.). To the latter, we owe the currently prevailing theory about the origin of the island's name. It is probably pre-Hellenic, and was derived from Andros or Andreas, son of Eurymachus or Anios and grandson of Apollo, to whom Rhadamanthus, brother of Minos gave the island. Poetic designations of the island testify to its lush vegetation and the abundant waters: Lasia, Nonagria, Hydrousa, Epagris. Its most ancient name was Gavros.

The earliest inhabitants of the island are reported to have been Pelasgians, Carians, Phoenicians and Cretans. In about 1000 BC, Andros was colonised by the Ionians. Archaeological finds on the island from the pre-historical period have been meagre. However, with regard to the Geometric and Archaic periods, significant information is being derived from the excavations of the Geometric town of Zagora. Excavations are still going on in the Ipsili region.

Zagora is situated on a remote and still fairly inaccessible promontory on the southwestern coast, on a site that is naturally fortified on the side of the sea. The excavations, along the section that links the promontory with the rest of the island, have unearthed a considerable part of the town, with private dwellings, a sanctuary and a temple as well as a fortification wall, among the most remarkable of the period. The gate in this wall is of special interest, as it was built using techniques similar to those used on the Lion Gate in Mycenae. Also, clay vessels have been found, metal objects, bone and stone votive offerings, stone implements and lamps, all revealing the level of the life and activity of the inhabitants of that age. The town was inhabited systematically from the late 10th century BC, a period that coincides with the arrival of the Ionians, but the identity of its founders remains uncertain. The period of its greatest prosperity was the second half of the 8th century BC (750-700 BC, the late Geometric period). The town was abandoned soon after 700 BC, with the exception of the sanctuary, which was still in use until the end of the 5th century BC. Its inhabitants moved to another site, but their ancestral worship (probably of Athena) remained in the same place.

Earthenware jar with relief Greek key decoration, 2nd half of 8th c. BC.

The good condition of the Zagora buildings allowed archaeologists to form a clearer idea of the ground plan of Geometric period dwellings in the

Hermes of Andros,
copy of the Praxiteles Hermes.
Archaeological Museum Andros,
Hellenistic period.

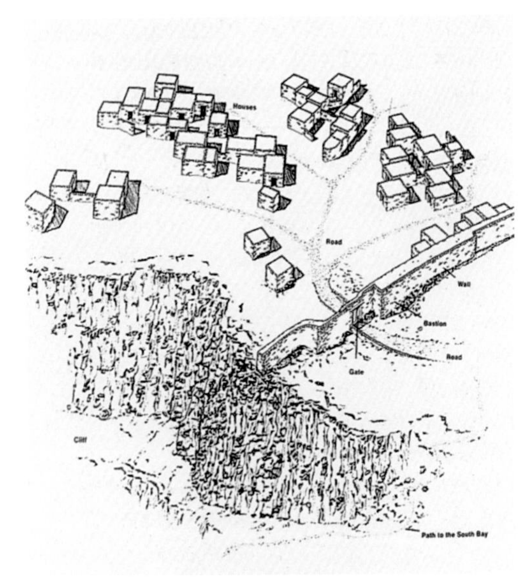

Artist's representation of the buildings of Zagora.

broader area of Greece as a whole. At the same time, significant similarities were discovered between the Geometric and the more modern traditional architecture of Andros settlements. All findings reflect the communication of the inhabitants with mainland Greece and the other islands.

The residents of Andros, Ionians and others who had become assimilated, were compassionate and ethical, and made a living by extracting iron, conducting trade and establishing (mid-7th century) colonies on Chalcidice (the settlements at Acanthus, Sani, Stagira – homeland of Aristotle – and Argilo have been confirmed). Up to the 6th century BC, Andros was an independent city-state that belonged to the ancient Amphictyony of Delos, centre of Sun worship. Of the 12 gods of Olympus, Dionysus was worshiped as patron of the island, and it was to him during his annual festival, that the miracle of the conversion of water to wine was attributed. (Philostratus). Also, Zeus Phratrius, Apollo Patrous, Athena Taurobolus and other gods were worshipped in particular on Andros. The inhabitants spoke the Ionian dialect. The first written monument of this age is regarded as being the epigraph "Zeus Meilichios", of the 7th century, which was found incised on a rock in the region of present-day Paleopoli.

Classical era

The founding of the ancient capital of Andros on the site of present-day Paleopoli is associated with the abandonment of Zagora and marks the beginning of the classical period. It contained a market, port (with visible traces), a citadel in a commanding position near today's little church of Ayios Dimitrios and, possibly, a theatre or stadium. The fact that the seat of an eponymous spectator has been found bearing the inscription Pythonymus Nicocratus argues for the existence of a theatre or stadium.

The wall around the settlement encompassed an enormous area. Its centre was on the Paleopoli plain, relatively close to the sea, and it was well fortified. Parts of the western wall remain clearly visible. Ancient remains (wall sections, epigraphs, parts of large structures, capitals, etc.) are scattered about and have obviously been damaged by the passage of time and exposure to the elements.

Systematic excavations began in 1956 when a considerable part of the ancient agora (market) was unearthed. Digging continued from 1987 on. Early Christian basilicas and inscriptions prove that the town existed at least as early as the 5th century AD. Other evidence indicates the existence of at least 50 settlements at various points on the island. Gavrio was an important port.

During the Persian Wars, Andros went over to the Persians. It remained under Persian domination until the naval battle of Salamis (480 BC). For this, Themistocles, winner of the battle, wanted to punish the Andriots by demanding money from them. The Andriots cited poverty and bewilderment; in short, their inability to pay, resulting in an unsuccessful siege of the town, which became the cause of hostility between the Athenians and the Andriots.

Andros initially joined during the First Delian League (478/477 BC), on condition that it give ships and men, but it was also obliged to pay the "island tax" (451 BC). To prevent rebellion, Athens sent 250 men to the island who had been allotted plots of land (437 BC), and behaved like conquerors.Things went from bad to worse at the outbreak of the Peloponnesian War, with the inhabitants of Andros as tributaries and obliged to follow the Athenians in their campaigns. Their desertion led Alcibiades to mount a campaign against Andros, but he too failed to capture the town.

The dominance of Sparta, which followed the Athenians' defeat in the Peloponnesian War, was repugnant to the Andriots so that Conon the Athenian was subsequently welcomed as a liberator (393 BC). From then on, Andros remained loyal to the Athenians, even when the Macedonians were trying to win allies. Later, the island distinguished itself in the battle of Chaeroneia (338 BC).

Menander's comedy Andria *was written at the end of the 4th century BC. From its Latin paraphrase, we learn about the simple and cordial manners of the Andriots. Sixty silver and bronze coins of the Andriot state have been found, some with beautiful depictions of the god Dionysus, bearing dates ranging between the 4th century BC and 212 AD.*

Hellenistic period

After the battle of Chaeroneia, Andros came under the rule of Philip and later of Alexander the Great. It remained under direct Macedonian rule until 315 BC, when the first Macedonian garrison was installed to guard Caphareus (now called Kafireas).

The hostility between the successors of Alexander the Great led to successive reconquests of the island by Egyptian and Macedonian kings with the result that the administration, the political system, the customs and cults all changed. In 200 BC, the raid of the Rhodians was repulsed, who then sought help from King Attalus of Pergamum and the Romans. That same winter, the Romans and Attalus landed troops at Gaurium (today Gavrio) and moved against the town. The Andriots barricaded themselves in the town with the Macedonian garrison, but surrendered on the third day. As a reprisal, they were exiled to Delios (today Dilesi) in Boeotia, under harsh conditions. Their island was laid waste and handed over to Attalus, who then permitted the return of the wretched inhabitants. The situation gradually improved.

The only significant monument from the Hellenistic period is the cylindrical tower of Ayios Petros, 20 metres high and 9.70 m. in diameter at the base. It once had five or six floors, but its upper sectionshave now been destroyed. A low opening (1.30 m.) to the south leads to the ground floor area, to a vaulted chamber in which another opening was concealed in a thick wall, and led by a spiral stone stairway to the upper floors. The base of the tower is built with huge boulders in the Pelasgian order, put together with no binding material in between. The main body of the tower also boasts exceptional material and structure. Unfortunately, no precise conclusions can be drawn as to the date of the monument or its function. It may have been a station for re-transmitting torch signals (phryktoria) *or a storage space for the ores exported from the region.*

Roman rule - Byzantine years

Direct Roman rule began in 129 BC, when Andros became part of the province of Asia. There was a period of instability with the frequent appearance of pirates, the civil wars between Roman governors and plundering. The majority of the inhabitants suffered poverty and high-handed actions against them; morals degenerated, Asian cults were introduced (there is an indicative inscription with a hymn to Isis which was found in Paleopoli) and it was not until the years of Hadrian and Trajan that Andros enjoyed better treatment.

In the early Byzantine years, the island remained under the administration of Asia. The sparse evidence from that period informs us of the gradual spread of Christianity, the existence of a significant neoplatonic philosopher (Proclus, 5th cent. AD) as well as of the participation of the Cycladic people in the uprising against the iconoclast emperor Leo III the Isaurian (727 AD). In the 8th and

9th centuries, Andros belonged to the man holding the military rank of drungarius *of the Aegean Sea and, owing to its significant geographical position with respect to Constantinople, it was the seat of an important official as well as of the imperial Customs.*

During the Byzantine period, the island was divided into three parts: Exo Merea (the northern side of Petalo), Mesa Merea (southern side of Petalo and northern Gerakonas) and Piso Merea (rest of the island). Memories of this division are retained in the place name Piso Meria. The most significant information about Byzantine Andros comes from the 9th century AD (early Byzantine humanism), the period when Leon the philosopher or mathematician came to the island from Constantinople with elementary education in order to study rhetoric, philosophy and mathematics under a wise man whose name is unknown to us.

Wall painting and exterior view of the church of Ayios Taxiarchis, Mesaria.

Then he visited the wealthiest monastic libraries of the period and arrived at a high level of knowledge.

Life on Andros was disrupted by Saracen pirate raids, but in particular by their installation on the island of Crete (826 AD), until the victory of the Byzantine fleet against them (908). They appeared later as well.

In the 12th century, we have the first indications of sericulture and the export of the famous silks (the hexamita *that were mainly produced on Andros and* zentata*), activities that brought prosperity to the island.*

At the same time however raids and attacks started coming from the West (Venetians, Normans, Genoans). There are some significant confirmed Byzantine monuments, mainly churches, that have been preserved and that we will see on our tours around the island. The study by D. Paschalis (1936) of the 12 Byzantine monasteries on Andros is based on field research and on manuscript evidence; but they were mainly later dependencies of the larger monasteries. What is lacking is systematic research on the fortified sites dating to the Byzantine period (Apano Kastro Kochilou, Paliopirgos Melidas, Pachikavos in the Korthi Gulf).

Venetian rule

After Constantinople fell to the Crusaders in 1204 AD, with an intervening period in which Andros was ruled directly from Venice, Marino Dandolo became its first ruler (1207). Three years later, he acknowledged the sovereignty of Marco Sanudo, duke of Naxos, in the Aegean.

Later, power devolved to the Sanudo family until the dynasty ended (1384), when the dynamic intervention of Francesco Crispo brought Petro Zeno to the fore. The latter was the most active and effective of the Venetian leaders in terms of his diplomatic skills, with prestige in both East and West. It appears that the island, which often suffered from raids by Genoans, Catalans and Turks, felt some security in Zeno's days.

The initiative of inviting Christian Albanian families (Arvanites) *from Attica and Evia to colonise the island was also attributed to him*
Their establishment in northern Andros reinforced the island both demographically and financially. The dynasty that was linked with the fate of Andros between the mid-15th century and 1566 came from the Somaripa family of Paros. During its rule, the Turkish threat appeared strongly. In 1540, Andros became a tributary of the Sultan, owing to the looming presence in the Aegean of the pirate Khair-ed-Din Barbarossa.

The last master of Andros, Giovanni Francesco Somaripa, was removed by the Andriots themselves, 9000 of them according to the report, because of the oppression of the island by 3000 Venetians. They put in a provisional government and called Piali Pasa (1566) to take the island, which in 1579 came directly under Turkish rule.

The Venetian princes and landowners laid the foundations for feudalism. This system expired inthe 17th century, but its influence on the Andros society was felt until much later.

In their great concern for defence, the Venetians built significant fortification works, such as at Apano Kastro (Upper Castle) in Kochilou, the largest and strongest, Kato Kastro (Lower Castle) in Chora (Andros town) and Castello de Ostodossia or Tower of Makrotantala on the northwestern coast of the island. Place names testify to the existence of smaller forts for local needs.

The establishment of the Western Episcopate of Andros (as early as 1208 AD) by the Latin Archbishopric in Athens marked the arrival of Western clergy and possibly the expulsion of senior Orthodox clergy from the island. Most of the Western-style churches, apart from that of Ayios Andreas (St Andrew) in Chora, have not been preserved.

1

Period of Turkish rule

(1566-Revolution 1821)

The way in which Andros passed over to Turkish rule benefitted it in terms of safeguarding significant privileges. For example, the Turkish authorities were forbidden to commit high-handed actions or to compel the islanders to convert to Islam; some taxes were abolished (inheritance tax, excise tax on silk, etc.) and property titles and contracts were recognised. The inhabitants could seek redress from the Porte, appoint sentries of their choice, wear the local dress, maintain their churches and monasteries, and observe their ancestral religion and customs. But the head tax, the tithe and other taxes were burdensome, and violations of privileges were not unknown.

Under Turkish rule, control of the island passed successively from the jurisdiction of the Turkish admiral of the fleet to the mother of the Sultan, to Russian administration (1700-1774, First Russo-Turkish war), to ownership by Sach Sultana (the Sultan's sister) who looked after the island and, finally, it devolved to the direct power of the financial authorities.

The highest office was held by the Aga, while the inhabitants were represented by the elders of the four residential and administrative regions that had come into being on Andros: Amolochos or Megalo Horio in northwestern Andros; Arna (today's Arni up to Batsi and Aprovato), Kato Kastro or Chora and the surrounding area, and Apano Kastro (Korthi region). The noble families of the island, mainly of Byzantine origin, came from the two latter regions. The highest office, in great demand, despite the risk it entailed in this form of local government from 1774 on, was the kotzambashi, who was responsible for collecting taxes. His election by acclamation took place at a mazoma (assembly of the population) at the alai of Panagia Vourgara in Mesaria, often in a highly charged atmosphere. Most of the elders were lords from Kato Kastro (Chora, Mesaria, Apatouria etc.). Trustees were appointed to assist them in other regions. Like all lords, they lived in fortified houses, held the most fertile lands, followed the inheritance law of the first-born – which led many second-born, dowerless children to the clergy or

1. What remains of the Kastro in the Kochilou region.
2. Marble icon from Amolochos (1780).

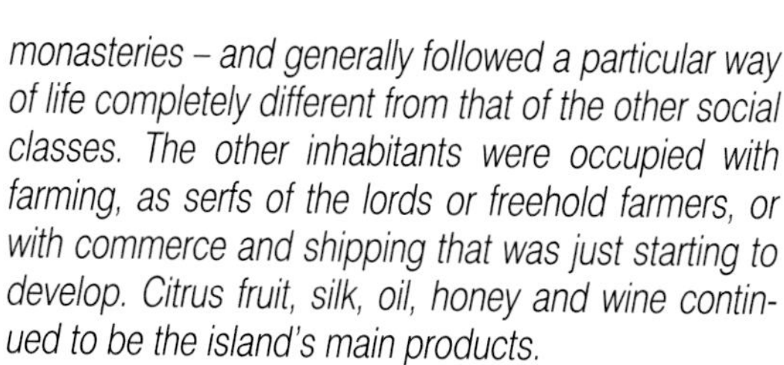

monasteries – and generally followed a particular way of life completely different from that of the other social classes. The other inhabitants were occupied with farming, as serfs of the lords or freehold farmers, or with commerce and shipping that was just starting to develop. Citrus fruit, silk, oil, honey and wine continued to be the island's main products.

The first information we have about the commercial shipping activity of the Andriots was given to us by the French traveller Jean de Thévenot in 1665, who wrote that silk was transported by ships built on Andros. But the real prerequisites for growth in this sphere were not secured until after the first Russo-Turkish war (1768-1774), when the Black Sea once again became accessible to Greek seamen. From the mid-18th century on, there were contracts for the buying and selling of ships or interests in them, to charters, bottomry, and demands for compensation (by ships' captains or reizidoi and partners or parsineveloi).

According to Pouqueville's list (1813), Andros had 40 sailing ships with a total of 2800 tonnage (average 70 tons), 400 seamen, 800 cannons and ranked fifth among the country's 26 ports in terms of numbers of vessels and 11th in tonnage. The town of Andros (Chora) was evolving gradually into a nautical society. Piracy never ceased to plague the island which, during the wars between Venice and Turkey (1664-1669, 1684-1699), suffered the vengeful wrath of the adversaries. In 1670 was the terrible sack of Chora by Hugo de Sevelier of France in particular. However, the Turks too were being harassed by pirates, especially those from Tinos, who would raid them after first conspiring with the Andriots. For this reason, the Turks were gradually obliged to abandon the island.

The establishment of schools is reported from the 16th century on. Special care was taken to re-establish the Episcopate of Andros in 1621, after which Orthodox monks began moving into the monasteries. The first school to offer classes in Greek was established in Chora during the period of Russian rule (1770-1774). By means of his own hard work and at his personal expense, the monk, teacher and missionary Samuel Plasimis or Skazis from Amonaklio established the "Greek Letters" school, also called the Holy Trinity School, in 1813-1818 in neighbouring Moskionas (former municipality of Korthi), in the precinct of a church by the same name. Many Andriots studied and taught in Kydonies, Smyrna, Constantinople and Walachia.

Modern period

Just before the Revolution in 1821, an intellectual climate had been created on the island that fostered the awakening of the Andriots: crews of Andriot and other sailing ships, through their voyages around the Mediterranean and Black Sea, acquired seafaring experience and a liberal spirit. The schools on Andros and in the colonies of the West, Asia Minor and elsewhere, remembering the past, transmitted enthusiasm about the idea of restoring the national identity of the Greeks. The Philiki Etairia, the secret society for promoting the Revolution against Ottoman rule, found a response in the Andriot community – especially among its leaders, clergy and teachers – as a result of which 37 Andriots were known to be members of the Etairia.

The Revolution was officially proclaimed on 10 March 1821 by Theophilos Kairis, after the divine service at the cathedral of Ayios Georgios (St George), Andros. A Revolutionary Assembly was convened, then a Revolutionary Trusteeship was set up by the elders of all regions of the island. Its first concern was to collect money to outfit the ships that would protect the island from the Turks of Karystos, a fact that made the seamen's role vital in decision-making. A large number of Andriot sailors served on ships from Hydra, Spetses, and Psara and many distinguished themselves as captains of fireships. Andriot ship owners took part in the blockade of Karystos.

The fact that many Andriots took part in operations wherever the Revolution was taking place bears witness to their vigorous patriotism. One characteristic example was that of the Trustee of Amolochos Giannoulis Dimitriou (1777-1857), the most active elder of the period. Also important was the financial support provided by the monasteries of Andros. From 1830 to 1850, the Andros sailing ships went through a stage of growth "so great that Andros has today become one of the most noteworthy parts of the Kingdom, for the wealth and prosperity of its inhabitants," according to a journalistic source of 1839.

Not only did shipping not hinder investments in land or the intensive cultivation of the island, in fact it provided the necessary capital for these projects. After 1850, ever larger ships were being registered for ever longer voyages, but some decline began when steam started to take over from sail (late 19th century), a change to which the ship owners of Chora, who were traditionally more active, adapted, with capital from the Andriot colony in Romania and other interested investors. The first Andros steamship was registered on 1st July 1882 by Vas. L. Empirikos and named after his main financier ("Skaramangas"). By 1914, there were 60 Andros steamships.

They made a significant contribution to the national struggles taking place then (1912-13, 1919-22). During the years 1923-27, in terms of registrations, Andros was the country's second

port after Piraeus. Bombing caused great losses of both ships (about 70 in all) and human lives during World War II. It is worth noting that the participation of Andros in national struggles is also associated with the name of colonel Antonios Kampanis (d. 1913) hero of the Balkan Wars. The period of Italian occupation (May 1941-September 1943) and the German occupation after that (up to 8 September 1944) were extremely difficult. The refusal of the Italians to hand themselves over to the Germans (1943) led to the bombing of Chora and the destruction of some of its most magnificent mansions (Empirikaika, Rivas and Plakouras).

Often during modern times, Andriots would find a solution to their problems of survival or their educational quests by migrating. In the 19th century, Constantinople, Smyrna, Kydonies and Alexandria – cosmopolitan centres accessible through the already familiar sea routes – but also Athens, Piraeus, and Hermoupoli on Syros, which was then developing, constituted important poles of attraction. In Romania and Crimea, Andriot enterprises flourished, particularly commercial ones. Also, in the early 20th century, a wave of migration toward the US and Canada lasted for many decades. After the war, however, even though living conditions were beginning to improve through public works owing to the bequests of ship owners and other Greeks living abroad, the population of Andros was rapidly abandoning the island. The high demands of many now well-to-do Andriots and the need for higher studies and jobs in new sectors, or even just the charm of the capital that is so close, created a wave of migrants toward the cities that can be seen up to the present day.

Engraving depicting Chora.

3

CULTURE & TRADITION

If you really want to understand a place, what you need to do, apart from direct observation, is find a way to reach into the past and find the conditions that influenced the views and habits of the inhabitants. For this reason, we are providing information here which, in conjunction with the facts of history, constitute a dynamic social and cultural framework in which the personality of modern Andros will be better understood.

To start with, it should be noted that even though there are close links between Andriots and Athenians, a good many local customs of greater or lesser significance are retained in Andros today. Many of them have been imprinted on the common Cycladic way of life and culture. Most of the 8000 current inhabitants of Andros, who have the privilege of living in a beautiful and safe place, have been witnesses to, although not always protagonists in, the battle of the past to survive and become a functional part of the present. Invaluable elements of the past are the unique architectural heritage, the trades, the arts and crafts, the musical and dance tradition, the linguistic idioms, the cultural events, the characteristic ideas and manners. Some have already been relegated to memory, while others, in their original form or adapted, can surprise the unsuspecting observer even today.

People and occupations

What mainly differentiates Andros is its maritime tradition that stems from both the innovative activity of Andriot ship owners since the late 19th century, and the zeal and enthusiasm shown by many generations of Andriots for the seaman's trade. Through the pages of history, we have seen the course charted by sail-powered shipping, which did not eliminate traditional occupations, but on the contrary, fostered them promoting the famous products of Andros (silk, lemons, meat, pulses, etc.) on markets in Greece and abroad.

The seaman's trade then attracted chiefly the residents of Kato Kastro (Chora) which on the eve of the Revolution was a shipping town. The changeover to steamships was crucial to the competitiveness of Andriot shipping, as well as that of Greece as a whole.

Among the protagonists of this change was Dimitrios Moraitis who, within ten years of his start in 1893, built 12 steamships with a total tonnage of 50,000 grt. To him Andros owes a significant first, the registration in its port, in July 1907, of the first Greek passenger ship, the ocean liner Moraitis *(later renamed* Themistocles*) that inaugurated the Greece-America line.*

Andriot shipowners bought many cargo ships after World War I, so that by 1928, Andros had 23% of all of Greek steam shipping. They reacted flexibly after World War II as well, when only ten Andriot ships were left. Large-scale purchases of ships followed (from 1950 on) and provided a solution to the acute problem of unemployment caused by the devastation of the war. After 1947, the purchase of the famous Liberty ships from the U.S. with government guarantees and on particularly favourable terms, saved the situation.

The now profitable seaman's trade acquired such prestige that it drew in almost the entire male population of the island, including men from the most traditional rural districts. Thus today, even in remote villages, one can encounter men who had "served" at sea. In first place is Stenies, a community known as a "captain's village", although the other villages in the region are not far behind. One does not have to be particularly familiar with the subject to be able to single out groups of veteran seamen with the proud bearing and nostalgia that can be felt behind their narrations of the hardships of life at sea.

The sea no longer constitutes the fate and exclusive destination of young men. Sooner or later the seaman's trade will also pass into the sphere of tradition, as have so many others.

The miller's trade, for example, belongs among those that have necessarily been abandoned. With it the crafts of the potter, silk farmer and textile weaver have also been lost. Even needlework can only be seen now in old-fashioned trunks or in the hands of older women.

Agriculture and animal husbandry, with which the older inhabitants of the island are usually occupied, can still be found. Their aim is to cover the needs of what are now small families. In addition, regions such as

Makrotantalo, Vitali, Arni, Vourkoti, Livadia, Korthi, etc. supply the local market with particular goods (potatoes, pulses, citrus fruit, meat, etc.).

Another "traditional" pursuit, practised by the island's older housewives is cheese-making, as well as cooking and confectionery in which all local products are utilised. Many men are now engaged with keeping bees and vineyards. Even the Andriots who live in Athens keep vineyards on the island, since it is easy for them to "pop over" on a weekend to prune, harvest, and press grapes, and make raki.

Animal husbandry is among the occupations that have not been abolished by tourism.

The village of Sineti has a long tradition and a high reputation for its wines. For the Andriot householder it is a source of joy and pride to be able to serve visitors his own wine, or his tasty raki and other homemade products. He never misses a chance to send such gifts to relatives and friends in Athens and elsewhere.

The curing of sausages and preserved pork meats has a special place in Andriot cooking. The process of preparing and preserving meat, which requires experience, the coordination of many people, patience and good spirits, is called hirosfagia *(pig-slaughter) or* gamos tou hirou *(wedding of the pig), since especially in the old days, it provided the occasion for a big party.*

1

Beekeeping and farming are among the Andriots' most popular occupations.

2

Today, even though self-sufficiency is not regarded as equally necessary, those who have the facilities, the means, the help and the disposition, repeat the ancestral ritual once a year (usually between October and December). The special outlet for this effort is the mayerio *(kitchen) in which nutritious and tasty foods are prepared using pork as a base. In the evening particularly, when there is widespread relief that the work is over, the meal is more official.*

The householder's wine flows in abundance and is accompanied by good wishes that the food thus prepared is "well eaten" and that the whole ritual is repeated "next year too".

Traditional preparation of cured pork.

Customs and manners

Traditional music and dances continue to be an integral part of a wedding celebration or a feast day. The purpose of dance groups in Andros or groups of Andriot dancers in Athens is to preserve the old ways. These groups also contribute to ensuring a good party, one that will last all night, up to the next morning.

Summer **festivals** *are most successful, when there are more people around, especially in the less tourist-oriented, mountain villages. The festival is an entire process centred round some religious feast, as long as there is a church of the same name in the village, or even a chapel. The feast starts from the vespers on the eve. On the day itself, a divine service is conducted, with a procession around the village and the breaking of bread. Families who are celebrating distribute homemade bread and their own wine or other beverage to guests. Then there are the "greetings" in the houses around the church, or in any houses in which the householder or his wife are celebrating their name day. The guests go from one house to another offering their "greetings" and best wishes to anybody celebrating their name day.*

The guests are offered beverages, mainly raki, and confections, marzipan (amygdalota), *sweet pies* (kaltsounia), *and shortbreads* (kourabiedes). *This is followed by a festive meal and, according to the mood, dancing until dawn. In the evening, people gather in the country centres that "put on a dance". In the old days, dances were held in the houses of those celebrating. Groups would dance to tunes they had "requested " earlier.*

Feastdays in the monasteries and at the Theoskepastou in Chora – whose feast is celebrated on the Saturday after the last Chairetismoi *(literally "Greetings", referring to a series of hymns to the Virgin in mid-Lent) – are held with great solemnity on Andros, with the whole village attending. In addition, many customs have been preserved in relation to the*

1,4. Scenes from a church feast day.
2. Offering a spoon sweet and a glass of raki are customary traditions on Andros.
3. Traditional dish..

4

Procession of the icon around Chora.

celebration of Easter.

Good Friday is a day of strict fasting. After the church service, groups of people visit different parishes on the island to venerate the flower-bedecked Epitaphia, which is a particularly pleasant custom now that it is easy to drive around.

When the Resurrection is celebrated in the evening of Holy Saturday and again on Easter Sunday, many regions observe the nationwide custom of fireworks, especially Chora, Livadia, Vrachno, Apikia but especially Stenies where, with carefully coordinated movements and discipline by the "leaders", groups of young people set off the famous maskoula, *which are iron pipes or fairly large old shells which the inhabitants fill with gunpowder, tap down with a piece of ceramic, paper, and stones and "plant" it in the ground on the safest sites. The minutes before they are set off have a particular emotional charge – the tension of a military preparation – that somehow justifies the persistence in retaining this custom.*

Finally, if nothing else, Easter on Andros means lambriatis *and lots of wine. Lambriatis is the stuffed lamb or goat roasted in the oven. Even today, many village ovens are lit especially for this purpose, as there is great nostalgia for many of the customs of the religious and social life of Andros, which have declined today and which generally shape a person's character: religious, hard-working, law-abiding, philosophical, hospitable, humorous. If one were to compare Andriot customs with comparable ones from other Aegean islands, one would not notice substantial differences, but rather differences of form. And one would note that these customs are fading for approximately the same reason: decline of the traditional style and preference for the middle-class, urban way of life. The losses would perhaps have been even greater if the people of Andros, even the most well-travelled, had not been of a somewhat conservative bent.*

Included among the customary features is the use of various idioms. These are mainly names given to types of flora and fauna, to occupations and products, to objects of everyday use, etc., that vary from one region to another in terms of pronunciation and syntax. A distinct accent with elements from the northern Greek idiom is characteristic of the inhabitants of Apano Kastro. Also of great interest for specialists is the degree to which the Arvanitiki (Albanian) dialect has been retained in northwestern Andros up to the present time, parallel to the Greek language (see period of Latin rule).

Unfortunately, however, these linguistic differences have provided the occasion for parochial arrogance on the part of some so-called "genuine" Andriots. Such views constitute a tradition more honoured in the breech than in the observance. Otherwise, Andros, as every homeland, belongs essentially only to those who love it.

Music and dance

In the old days, one could usually find a self-taught musician and an enthusiastic singer or dancer among any group of people in a village. There were many opportunities for showing such skills: at hirosfagia, vengeres *(friendly gatherings in houses), and of course in the obvious places such as weddings and baptisms, name days and local feasts, and at jolly carnival parties.*

The musical instruments played on Andros were the violin with the lute or the santouri *– the latter more frequently in eastern Andros – and the* tsambouna *(symphonia) with the* toubi *(a wind instrument), the island* askavlos *(a bagpipe-type instrument), and percussion. The tsambouna was also played in Korthi. And whenever no musical instrument could be found, enthusiasm easily transformed some ordinary object into one.*

Songs with a 15-syllable line were reminiscent of the songs that could be heard more generally in the Aegean Sea. Many of them were improvised, inspired by the mood of the moment and the occasion. Typical songs about exile abroad, love lyrics, teasing songs, etc. were collected "from the mouth of the people" by Dimitris Paschalis, between 1885 and 1902. The lyrics below have been taken from this collection, and are indicative of the lives of the inhabitants.

Traditional dancers.

Go my voice to the sea and sail like a star
Go and bring greetings to my white lily

In addition to couplets, there were longer folk songs, songs about historic events, paraloges (narrative songs with fictitious content) and lullabies. A folk lament for Good Friday has also been found that was sung by women around the Epitaphios. Also, many Andriots remember Ayios Vassilis (the Greek equivalent of Santa Claus), and the local New Year's carols that have been neglected in favour of the few, less expressive, commonplace lyrics of the "national" carols. Vocal abilities and a special mood were required, especially to sing the long, slow love songs (amanedes). The singer with a grievance and in a philosophical mood could "disrupt" the cheerful party atmosphere in the wee hours – a change that was reflected by the musicians and dancers:

A black rock on the shore will be the pillow
beneath my head, because whatever the
body suffers is the head's fault

Folk and Smyrnaian songs that had become known through the cultural exchanges created by sea voyages were also popular.

The dances that were constantly danced on Andros were the syrtos *(round) and the balos (either slow or fast). Less widespread were the Asia Minor dances (*karsilambas, hasapiko, *etc.). The cosmopolitan Andriots, however, incorporated foreign dances such as the foxtrot, tango and waltz into their parties. Although the syrtos and the balos were danced throughout the*

Cyclades, the way in which they were danced differed from one island to another.

On Andros, the traditional dance was relatively modest and simple – and highly expressive for precisely this reason.

The dancers are upright and proud, they "balance" their arms nicely and avoid exaggerated movements. The syrtos can be danced by men and women alike, or just by men. In the former case, in the tsalimia, *the first man or woman leads, although an informal code imposes coordination, the rest may also take part with some special steps. Popular old syrtoi are the Politikos, Sylivrianos, "the old woman's castle", Korthiani, and others. The men form a circle by themselves holding each other's shoulders, with moments of particularly high spirits, when the slowest tunes were played: "Asizies", "Kitsou i mana", "Potamos" and others. Their dance then becomes more spontaneous, and their expression is liberated.*

Now everybody (and not just the first dancer) can do the tsalimia, while interjections and the characteristic rhythmic stamping of the feet are heard frequently.

The Andriot balos is a gentle game of exchanging messages of love, and owes its charm to the rhythmically harmonised movement of the dancers in the more caring, less aggressive "ring" formed by body of the dancer around his lady, in the modesty of both, in the exchange of glances. The melodic tunes of the balos help in particular with their slight variations in tempo, and are played in a distinctive way from one island to the other. More or less lively, less lyric, and more enthusiastic is the fast balos (sousta), *usually a continuation and conclusion of the slow one.*

It has been argued that the balos "came" to Andros from the West during the period of Venetian rule. The transition from a group round dance to facing couples is a commonplace in traditional dancing in all regions of Greece, and in fact serves the essential human need for erotic expression and communication during periods when social conventions were quite strict. At dances on Andros, people actually met, or interested parties tried to impress each other or to charm. Thus, up until recently, dances were "responsible" for most siaximata *(engagements).*

Arts and Letters

When trying to become better acquainted with a place, it is worth learning some facts about selected Andriots who distinguished themselves in the intellectual realm.

Theophilos Kairis

One of the figures who left their mark on the intellectual horizon of 19th century Greece was undoubtedly Theophilos Kairis (Andros 1784 – Syros 1853). From the age of eight years old, he assiduously sought knowledge at the famous Kydonies School that belonged to Gr. Sarafis and Benjamin Lesvios on Patmos, on Chios and, as a monk from 1801 on, in Pisa and Paris, where he is associated with Adamantios Korais and other European thinkers. He offered his services for a year to the Evangelical School in Smyrna. Then he undertook, with great success, the directorate of the "Ellinomousio" in Kydonies (1812-1821), teaching physics, mathematics, philosophy and looking after its scientific equipment. He joined the Philiki Etairia in 1819 with a monumental speech proclaiming the freedom of the island of Psara, signalled the start of the Revolution on Andros and visited other islands. With his personal authority, he fought against the discord in the Peloponnese and took part with self-denial in the expedition of Olympus (1822), where he was wounded. He represented Andros continuously at the Assemblies of the Struggle and spoke frankly in his welcome to the governor Capodistrias (1828). He promoted the establishment of an orphanage for Andros children who were orphaned by the independence struggle, seeking contributions in Greece and abroad, and following personally every phase of the realisation of his plan. In 1835, the Orphanage was opened, and rapidly became a famous school with students from all over Greece and abroad. He himself taught literature, philosophy, metaphysics, rhetoric, poetics, mathematics, physics and astronomy. He looked after the children with fraternal devotion while living an ascetic life. He did not hesitate, while teaching his pupils religion and fear of God, to take his religious sentiment onto roads beyond the Orthodox faith that he apparently served. He regarded any faith other than faith in God "vain, disastrous and hubristic", as it created arbitrary types of religion (rituals, prayers, psalms, division of time, etc.). He honoured doctrine, became dogmatic and a teacher of correct speech, and remained a mystic. He refused to make an avowal of Faith to the Holy Synod so his School was closed. He himself was confined to the monasteries of Skiathos and Thera, where his health broke down. He was exiled to Western Europe and returned after the Constitution was passed (1844). He was accused anew of proselytising and stood trial in 1852. His conviction and the heartlessness of state functionaries led him to death in the Syros prison (1853); his burial was an offence to human dignity. A few days later, the Supreme Court issued a ruling acquitting him of the charges. In May 1912, his memory was honoured in Andros by the unveiling of a bust in the square named after him in Chora.

Evanthia Kairi (1779 - 1866)

Evanthia Kairi, younger sister of Theophilos Kairis by 15 years, is among the distinguished Greek women of the 19th century. With her brother, she acquired a significant education, and in fact became the principal of the Girls' School in Kydonies. With the encouragement of her brother and Adamantios Korais, she began writing, mainly for patriotic and educational purposes. Her drama Nikiratos, about the fall of Mesolonghi, was performed in the Apollon theatre in Hermoupoli in 1829 and was later translated *into Italian. Having settled in Syros she established the First Girls' Elementary School, in which she was taught and was principal.*

Dimitris P. Paschalis (1865 - 1944)

Dimitris Paschalis was the Andriot who made it a fundamental goal in life to conduct comprehensive historical research and write a book about Andros, and actually achieved his aim.

He was born in Chora where he lived during his childhood. Later he went to Athens for high school and university (law) studies. From 1890 on, with a break between 1902-1924, during which he served as prefect in various prefectures, he occupied himself with historical research on Andros.

He utilised many different sources (earlier writers, ancient coins etc., findings from his own archaeological research, Byzantine monuments, manuscripts of all types, and testimonies from his contemporaries) and from 1898 on, began to publish his papers. His works fall into two categories: extensive and independent, and shorter studies of specific themes. For example, "The History of Andros", "Andros during the Revolution of 1821", "Theophilos Kairis", etc. belong to the first category.

The second includes a multitude of monographs of historical, linguistic, folkloric, literary, and legal interest, biographies, and bibliographical guides, all shedding light on the history and cultural level of Andros. As a tribute to his contribution, the Academy of Athens made him a corresponding member.

Vassilios Tatakis (1896 - 1986)

Strangely unknown on Andros, Vassilis Tatakis is one of the most important modern Greek philosophers. He was born in Sineti. He studied literature in Athens and philosophy at the Sorbonne, where he was awarded the degree of Doctor of Philosophy.

He worked zealously in secondary education, even though he suffered "unforgivable persecutions, accumulated injustice" on the pretext of his linguistic convictions (champion of the demotic language). He became an educational consultant in 1945 and was elected professor of philosophy at the University of Thessaloniki in 1958.

He wrote some important books: His Byzantine Philosophy *was the first systematic study in the global literature on the theme, which had been underestimated until then. He continued to write books, dictating them when his eyesight failed. Many people who knew him considered him "a philosopher who believed in human virtue".*

Mikhail Th. Tombros (1889 - 1974)

M. Tombros was from a large Korthian family of marble carvers. He himself was born and lived for the greater part of his life in Athens, where he died, leaving behind a significant body of work (mainly sculptures in marble, bronze, plaster of Paris and clay), which brought him many distinctions. Among others, there was the occasion n 1959 at the unveiling of the stature of the Unknown Sailor, for which he received the Commander of the Phoenix medal. He took part in many international exhibitions. His works can be divided into two categories: the "conventional" sculptures (busts, statues of people, memorials) which he would create upon commission, and his "free compositions", through which he showed himself to be the main vehicle of the innovative Parisian movements of the interwar period.

His creations can be seen mainly in the Museum of Modern Art in Andros, in museums and art galleries of Athens, as well as in other public areas of Greece and Cyprus.

Andreas Empirikos (1901-1974)

Andreas Empirikos, son of ship owner Leonidas Empirikos, was born in Braila, Romania. He was a cosmopolitan person as well as being a devotee of Andros, which is why he visited the island frequently during his early years.

His first collection of poetry, a landmark, was "Ipsikaminos" (Blast furnace), a "scandal and an act of heroism in the Greek letters of 1935", which constituted, according to M. Vitti, the most genuine experience of surrealism in Greece.

Memorial to the "Unknown Sailor" in Chora.

At the same time he was writing "Endohora" (Hinterlands), in which Empirikos showed himself to be less of a surrealist but more of a poet. In 1951 he completed his prose "Megas Anatolikos" on Andros, which was not published until after his death.

In this book he praises beauty everywhere as well as free love, a fact which often provided critics an excuse to condemn his work.

Andreas Karantonis (1910 - 1982)

Andreas Karantonis was born in Lamira. He was a poet, but mainly a literary critic, the most important of the 1930s generation.

At the age of 19 years old, he published his first critical study. He also wrote long poems and essays in which he refuted materialist and totalitarian theories. Karantonis was the editor of the literary magazine Nea Grammata *from whose pages he openly supported the use of the demotic language.*

Architecture

Another way of getting to know Andros is of course to approach its vernacular architecture, a group of functional structures (places of worship, various types of dwellings, ancillary buildings, and technical projects), whose aesthetic quality is as high as its technical workmanship. In these buildings, it has been shown that the accumulated experience of centuries, dating back to the geometric age, has been preserved. This was what dictated conformity with the configuration of the terrain, with climatic conditions, with the special features of the local materials (schist, clay, cypress wood) and made it possible to adapt them to the practical needs of the inhabitants, as well as making them into a medium for artistic creation.

Settlements were usually built at various altitudes on slopes with a steep gradient – decisive factors in their street plans. Thus, the arrangement of buildings in a straight line is rare; more frequent and more spectacular, is the amphitheatrical layout. For communication between private and public spaces, a labyrinthine network of stone-paved streets is created, frequently steep and with many stairs. These lead to the once vital points of the village: to the springs, usually more than one - that were decisive to the existence of a settlement and to serving household needs before water supply networks came into being – or to established gathering places. These places were the parish churches with the little squares around them, and the coffee shops and little stores. Communication between the various regions of Andros was maintained for centuries by a network of mule tracks, most of which were stone paved and well looked after (e.g. from Chora to Korthi, from Arni to Chora, etc.).

Criteria for selecting sites and building a settlement, apart from the existence of springs, included the distance from fertile lands and the protection from the north winds which are

1

2

strong and cold in winter.

Care was also taken with respect to the individual buildings. For example, houses were usually built so that their facade faced south or east, never north, even if the north side looked out onto the road. On the north face, windows are visibly smaller than those on the rest of the house. For the same reason, in many regions (e.g. Makrotantalo, Fellos, Korthio, etc.) a special type of threshing floor was built, and some have been preserved to this date, with a gardi*, i.e. an elevated wall on the north side. This wall had openings in it in which the farmers would place brush or branches as required, to modify the strength of the wind.*

Care was also taken to mitigate the blinding Aegean light. Most windows were of relatively limited dimensions, while on most farmhouses, there was an anentrada *i.e. a vine whose leaves effectively shaded the avli (courtyard).*

The villages on Andros today - especially those that have preserved the core of the traditional settlement or have taken into consideration aesthetic and functional needs in enlarging it - owe their picturesqueness largely to their proper adaptation to the environment. But the individual morphological elements we encounter in houses with their ancillary structures in rural villages or coastal towns, on farms or public lands also contribute greatly. Playing a leading role everywhere, since the era when Zagora and Ipsili were built, is the abundant schist rock and the characteristic way of building walls with this stone.

Specifically slabs of schist were cut to be as rectangular as possible in shape and placed with their long side horizontally. In the intervening spaces, smaller, flat unworked stones were carefully wedged, and instead of mortar, selected sieved soil was used. Needless to say, more care was used on the masonry for houses, especially on fortified houses and defence walls, e.g. around monasteries. On the contrary, less care was given to the way kellia *(small storage huts or stables) and* konakia *(small farmers' huts) were built on their lands.*

*A technique similar to that of masonry walls was used in building Andriot bridges, as well as the interior support arches in the houses (*volto *or arch). The same type of construction was also used to build* paravoles *or aimasies, which on Andros are the walls built by farmers around their fields to retain the accumulated soil, to enrich the land and to increase the arable area. Paravoles even raised slopes with a great incline to a workable level. The plots of land between paravoles are also called aimasies, each of which succeeds the other rhythmically and calmly.*

A fascinating detail is that the word aimasia can be encountered as early as

3

4

1. Example of traditional architecture in Giannisaio.
2. Convent of Ayia Eirini.
3. Threshing floor with a gardi*, a high wall on the north side for protection against the wind.*
4. Bridge over the Aladinos.

Homer, where it means the same thing as in the Andriot idiom, i.e. the paravoli, proving that the techniques and words that describe them have been in continuous use for millennia.

Thinner, dry stone walls were built to fence land. Large slate slabs were used to achieve economy of time, effort and materials, and placed upright between sections of dry wall (stimes or stimata).

This humble functional structure also has a remarkable aesthetic value thanks to the regularity of the distances, the calm contrast between vertical and horizontal lines and, of course, the fact that these walls snake over the entire surface of the island.

*1,2. Traditional Andriot walls with horizontal and vertical slabs (*stimata*).*
*3. Small earthenware jars (*bournies*).*
4. Wine barrels.
5. Traditional oven.

A. The House

The most composite structure, and therefore most indicative of a way of life for generations of people, is the house.

In terms of form, we can distinguish the old rural house, the tower (tower house), the mansion and the house in the newer towns (Gavrio, Batsi, Korthi Bay). Chora is small but charming, according to the stages of its expansion.

The rural house was a way of life for the Andriot, who had been a farmer for centuries, either a freeman or a serf on the few large estates of Frankish and Turkish feudal lords, as well as a tenant of Andriot nobles. He worked primarily to cover his family's needs, and when circumstances permitted, in the export trade. For example, even the construction worker, potter, and seaman, in order to be regarded as a worthy "householder", had to produce the products that would secure comparative self-sufficiency for his family, who of course took an active part in the effort. Functionally, the house had to play two roles: as residence for the large family and as a storeroom. The rural house can be divided into two basic types: a) that of a multi-unit plastic synthesis whose characteristic feature was the existence of more than one structural volume, one of which was discreetly emphasised, and b) the type of linear arrangement of space, known as makrinari *or wide-fronted house.*

The ground floor (katoi) *was used as storage space* (sodiastiko) *where the* tzares *(large earthenware containers with relief "rings" on their surface) containing the* gennimata *i.e. oil and wine were kept. Also kept in the storage area were* bournies *(small earthenware jars) containing pork or* kopanisti *(savoury "bournia cheese"), livestock feed, the implements of the rural life and work, the winepress, the cauldron for making raki, and wood for the hearth. Frequently, domestic animals were stabled in separate adjacent spaces. There were two stairways leading to the upper floor* (anoi), *the pre-eminently residential space: the external stairway, more carefully built, and frequently flanked by whatever could be used as a flowerpot (broken earthenware jars,*

3

4

5

1

large square tins, pails, etc.) - since Andriot women have always had a weakness for flowers – and the humbler, more utilitarian interior stairs. A few steep steps built into the wall led from the katoi to an opening in the upper floor that was covered by a wooden, unseen katapakti (trapdoor). For informal visits, people entered from the mayeirio (kitchen), while on feast days and other formal occasions, they would go directly to the sala, the "good" living room. The avli (courtyard) was certainly preferable on summer evenings. For casual cooking over a wood fire, a high kaminada (hearth) or mayirioulaki (little kitchen) was built in one corner of the yard (some can still be seen on houses in Arni). Also essential to the avli were pangalia, benches built round the walls, and a large number of galachtismenes (whitewashed) rocks. Today, especially in spring, one can gaze out onto the horizon from these splendid avles, through a frame of greenery. Carnations and basil are among the favourite plants, and the yards in higher villages are decorated with large earthenware jars filled with gardenias or spectacular hydrangeas. A typical feature of the Cycladic house generally is its flat roof, called a doma. On Andros, we encounter it on the oldest and most authentic examples of vernacular architecture.

To build this roof, parallel beams of durable cypress wood were placed to rest on the finished walls. Schist slabs or reeds were laid across the beams to fill in the gaps. Seaweed or brush would be spread over this as insulation, and covered by three layers of a particular red soil or clay. The artisans took special care in the final phase, where the sifted earth was dampened, and then kneaded with the feet and allowed to dry, or "crack". In a few days, the cracks were filled with more soil and the surface was dampened once again for the first biliasma, i.e. the spreading with a stone or marble cylinder (voli or bilia). Soon after came the second and third coat. From then on, every 2-3 years the householder had to repeat the biliasma, in order to keep the roof in good repair.

There are still a few old rural houses that attractively combine a flat roof with ceramic tiles or have just a tile roof.

We encounter aesthetic and functional harmony in many other external features of the traditional house, such as:

a) the special manner of plastering, the so-called sardeloma, popular to this day, where the plaster is "combed" giving the impression of wavy exterior surfaces. In other cases, the plaster emphasises the outline of the stone.
b) the whitewashing that permits chiaroscuro, as well as the contrast between whitewashed and "bare" surfaces (in katoyia, huts, ovens, etc.)
c) the faltsogonies, (literally "false corners") where the corners of houses were cut away to permit heavily loaded pack animals to walk through the narrow streets.
d) the kapaso, the symmetrical outside part of the chimney that decorated the roof.
e) the kornizakia or fteromata, slight outcroppings from the flat roof, to protect the plaster from the rain, and the kanalo (mouth) of the open gutter, both exclusive features of the Andriot house.

But since the rural house was and still is the focal point of social life on Andros, it was built *with rooms spacious enough to allow people to gather in them: the living room and kitchen. All the other spaces were palpably smaller, to the point that, instead of a bedroom, there would be a "bedplace", an opening in the wall slightly larger than the dimensions of a bed. The kitchen (mayeirio) was the most familiar place, much frequented but always tidy.*

2

3

1. *The plaster is protected from rainwater. by the* kornizakia, *outcroppings from the flat roof.*
2. *The lack of amenities stimulated the imagination and niches in walls were transformed into cupboards or shelves for plates.*
3. *Example of a* stamnothiki.

4., 5. *Details from a living room and a kitchen.*

4

5

Simple practical devices supplemented the lack of what are today self-evident comforts. There was the hearth (kaminada) for cooking and heating. When it occupied a larger space, and stools or rough benches (kromousia) could be placed beside it, it was called a tzakotopos. Niches in the thick stone walls were usually draped with embroidered cloths and used as cupboards (thourides). There was also a stamnothiki, i.e. a place where the water jar could be safely kept. Sometimes the wood-burning oven would be built inside the house in the kitchen or in an outside kitchen near it. When an interior space was especially large, an arch or volto would be built.

The living room (sala), high-ceilinged and spacious, was the most carefully furnished room in the house, in which the best embroideries, the family photographs, souvenirs from seamen's voyages or from family members living abroad, if any, were all displayed proudly. It was opened only on special occasions. On the upper floor there were large grills for keeping silkworms.

People today are surprised to see that every room is directly connected to the one beside it, and how thick the walls are (outer walls can be up to 1 metre thick), since this was the only type of thermal insulation.

Andros is fortunate in that these buildings have been preserved to this day. The island's low frequency of earthquakes has certainly contributed to this. There are moreover a good many families who still live in their ancestral houses, after making the necessary improvements. Totally modern structures are largely made to conform to the precepts of vernacular architecture.

Weathering is a great threat to those "towers" that have been preserved in Apatouria, Mesaria etc. They are massive, usually plain, three-storey structures of the fortress-type. The walls, especially on the ground floor are up to 3 metres thick, and the few small windows are protected by iron grilles. In order to ward

1

2

3

4

off pirate raids, there were loxikes *(gun emplacements) on the katoi,* thermistres *(built funnels for pouring down boiling liquids) over the fortified main door, and* masgalia *(machicolations) on the roof to provide protection for anyone shooting from there. More generally, the towers were not accessible to anyone who did not have specific business with the lord or who did not belong to the same class as he did. Women lived a restricted and monotonous life. They watched life go by through the windows built specially for them, which were spacious on the inside, with a double sill and benches for them to sit on when embroidering. Additional examples of the special nature of their inhabitants are the private chapels located alongside the towers.*

More recent buildings than these (period of late Turkish rule) and more attractive in appearance, since they are not in the heavy fortress style, are the arhontika *or mansions. Most of them were built in what was always the traditionally wealthiest district of Hora.*

The newest of the traditional settlements on Andros, that is Gavrio, Batsi, and Korthi Bay, were created after liberation from Turkish rule, when the inhabitants felt safe enough to settle in coastal locations and to take up trade and fishing. Many of them of course became seamen. Although, to date, the Andriots have not completely abandoned agricultural occupations, the rural house has been simplified on plan (square) and has acquired a terracotta tile roof. Open spaces and ancillary buildings have been limited, as habitation is denser, and larger windows have been built overlooking the sea. The tile roof has become the rule ' in the villages where the greatest return to the seaman's trade has been noted (Stenies, Sineti, etc.). Also, door and window frames and walls are painted in various shades, in other words, on Andros an architectural style has emerged that is unique in the Cyclades, and as attractive as the older form.

B. Watermills, dovecotes, fountains

Other special buildings on Andros that add to its distinct appearance are watermills, dovecotes and fountains. **Watermills** *were used on Andros more than windmills. Some lovely groups have been identified in Frousaii, Vitali, Katakilo, Kaparia, Piso Meria, Mesa Rogo, Dipotamata, Menites, and Stravopouries. Groups with fewer units or isolated mills exist in many other places. They belong to the Greek (or eastern) type with a horizontal* fteroti *(wheel), and consist of a tower* (kremasi) *and a main building, divided into two levels. The tower is a narrow, square structure rising over the main building. When the grinding mechanism was to be used, the water that had been collected in the* havousa *(tank) was channelled toward the tower, filtered and directed to the kanalo, the vertical opening in the tower. The grinding machinery was on the upper level of the main building and would be regulated by the miller according to his customers' requirements. The wheel was in the basement (katoi), and the water from the kanalo would fall on it with enough pressure to move it. The last mills were still in operation until about 1920. Some operated illegally during the Nazi occupation, despite the ban, to cover the people's needs for flour.*

1, 2. The mansions of Chora readily remind us of the features that many visitors have attributed to Andros, an old-world nobility.

3. The Kairis Tower.

4. Example of a fteroti water mill.

It has been said that the **dovecote** *is the most lyric, plastic structure in our vernacular architecture. Even though it has a very specific, practical use, it seems that the anonymous artisan preferred its limited surfaces to liberate his imagination and pleasure in his work in a way that provokes our admiration even today. Although dovecotes can be seen everywhere, most of them are in the Korthi region*

They are two-story structures, square on plan with a flat roof. On the upper floor (anoi) are the doves' nests, while the katoi is used as a storeroom. Because of the material (thin pieces of slate), geometric shapes predominate as decorative features (triangles, squares, diamonds, circles, etc.). The ratios of void and solid are retained carefully so that finally the decoration looks like "embroidery on a white canvas". At the corners of the roof, little columns are sometimes built to emphasise the metaphysical nature of the structure. To show off the forms to their best advantage, it is important for the building to be whitewashed.

***Fountains** and **springs** can be found everywhere on Andros. It is always a pleasant surprise to find them in every village or hamlet, on pasturelands, and in monastery precincts. As charming as they are functional, they are stone structures in various forms and dimensions that surround the waterspout, the* bousounari. *This is a stone or marble duct or, in some cases, the mouth of a marble lion's head. The water spills into a trough from which it is sometimes channelled into cisterns in order to water the fields. In the simplest cases, the stone structure is limited to the area around the bousounari. In villages, one is more likely to encounter roofed fountains that are square on plan, with a vaulted or square opening. Larger fountains have benches offering rest, as well as special, large basins for washing clothes.*

Springs and fountains on Andros confirm the possibility of harmony between aesthetics and functionality.

The Monasteries and Convents of Andros

The Zoodochos Piyi or Ayias Convent

This was once the most important monastery on Andros, with a major contribution to the local economy, as well as to the national liberation effort. It stands imposingly over the Kapsorahi area near Batsi. Nobody knows exactly when it was built, but the oldest written evidence of its age is the date 1325, on the Zoodochos Piyi (Font of Life) icon of the Virgin. Testimony to the period of its great prosperity (when it had dependencies all over the island and elsewhere) can be found in the surviving artefacts and written records. Standing in the courtyard, one is impressed by the beauty and harmony of the buildings. The doorframe of the katholikon (main church) and the north side of the wall, with its arches, its vaulted cloister, and outdoor stairs are examples of the distinct plasticity of the island. Inside the church, which belongs to the domed cross-in-square type, with a splendid carved wood sanctuary screen, are some wall paintings dating to the 14th and 16th centuries. The relief on the fountain beside the church is a rare example of ecclesiastical art of this type. Since its repair in 1928, the monastery has been operating as a convent, and has a reputation for excellent work in weaving. It is advisable to consult the abbess before visiting the convent.

1

1, 2. The Zoodochos Piyi or Ayias Convent.
3. 4. The Panachrantos Monastery.

2

Monastery of Panachrantos or Ayios Panteleimon

This is one of the most remarkable monasteries on Andros. It is located on a precipitous site called Katafygio (Refuge) ton Gerakonon, a name that may be derived from the word gerax *referring to the old hermits' cells that can be seen on the surrounding rocks.*

Tradition associates the foundation of the monastery with the successful Cretan campaign of the Byzantine commander-in-chief Nicephorus Phocas (10th century), but the historical accuracy of the written evidence is disputed. Earlier the icon of the Virgin, (Panachrantos) a work by the Apostle St Luke, appeared miraculously on the point where the chapel of Photodotis (Light-giver) is situated today. According to the Great Codex of the Monastery, in 1705 monks from this monastery purchased a relic, the skull of St Panteleimon, and brought it to the monastery where it is kept until this day. This explains the origin of the second name.

Well-kept and hospitable, the monastery attracts many pilgrims today. To visit it, one is advised first to consult the abbot. Here one is impressed by the site with its superb view, the interior and exterior spaces with the plane trees, springs, and arches over the various openings, and its cubic volumes which, owing to the limited space, are articulated on different levels around the katholikon. Rising up over them is the bell tower, the shape of which echoes the grace of Cycladic architecture. The katholikon is a small church in the Byzantine order with an octagonal dome. The exterior is revetted with schist and the lintel bears the sculpted representation of the Annunciation of the Virgin. Two wonderful 18th century wall paintings have been preserved in the vestibule. In the main church very few wall paintings have been preserved, but there is a splendid carved wood screen the lower parts of which are covered with multicoloured Rhodian tiles. The icon of the Panachrantos, with a silver cover and heavy with votive offerings, can be seen at the southern door to the Sanctuary. To the left, the icon and relic of the healer St Panteleimon are the pride of the monastery and

3

4

of the entire island. In the upper parts of the monastery is the chapel of St Panteleimon, as well as that of St Nicholas and John the Divine, with a beautiful marble templon, or sanctuary screen. Here, exorcisms are carried out. Also, the cell can also be seen in which the popular monk Christophoros Papaloukas spent the last years of his life (1854-1861), by order of the Holy Synod. Outside the monastery walls is the little chapel of the Photodotis, with cross vaulting which is rarely encountered on the islands. The disproportionately large bell tower stands out, and the marble doorframe and lintel lend it a strange grandeur.

Monastery of Ayios Nikolaos Neos

The Monastery of Ayios Nikolaos Neos of Vouvena (St Nicholas the New from Vouvena), was founded in the 11th century, was abandoned and re-established between 1450 and 1480 by some persecuted monks and was renovated in 1760. Today one is impressed by its particularly well cared for and devout environment. Arriving in the forecourt, one sees plane trees and a fountain. The interior of the complex, with its arches, bell tower, and the familiar plasticity of Andriot monasteries, is elaborately structured and shown off to ever better advantage by its successful restoration efforts.

The atmosphere of the monastery's principal church, built according to tradition by Chiot craftsmen, is evocative. The relic of the holy martyr St Nicholas, who was put to death in 720 AD at Vounena in Thessaly, is kept here. In the vestibule, we look with awe upon the icon of St Nicholas that belonged to the Bishop of Myron in Lycia in the 17th century, which was embroidered by the nun Leontia using hair from her own head instead of thread, in fulfilment of a promise. Another point of reference is the miraculous scented icon of the Virgin Root of Jesse or Blacherna, which has been in the monastery since the 15th century, when it was brought there by holy fathers from the famous church of the Virgin of Blacherna in Constantinople. Regarding another icon of the Virgin (in the vestibule, to the left of the entrance to the main church), the dry lilies that permanently flank it are said to blossom once a year (2 July). The memory of St Nicholas the New is honoured on 9th May. Interested persons can plan their visit by phone.

Monastery of Ayios Nikolaos Neos.

The Convent of Ayia Eirini

The convent of St Irene is between Apikia and Vourkoti, on the Archontas site. It was established in 1793 by the priest-monk Leontios Perrakis, son of Spyridon, from Apatouria. It was an elaborate, costly structure with a double precinct and marble members (bell tower, templon, floor with the double-headed imperial eagle in the centre) that was dissolved by decree during the reign of Otho in 1834. The church of the same name is preserved in good condition, in contrast with the outer buildings, which have collapsed. In the inner precinct, there is a spring with flowing water regarded as having medicinal properties.

Convent of Ayia Marina

The convent of St Marina was established in the 17th century on the site of an earlier church of the same name. It is a remarkable structure, surrounded by high walls. In earlier times it could accommodate more than 100 nuns. It was dissolved in 1834 by decree of the Viceroy, but the inhabitants of Apikia and the nuns did not permit its vessels and artefacts to be auctioned. Today even though there are no nuns or monks in the buildings, it nevertheless is cared for by an abbot, who serves as priest at Aladino, and by private persons, so that the site is clean and shows its island character to best advantage. The feast of St Marina (17 July) is commemorated here.

Monastery of Tromarchion (Virgin Tromarchiani)

This monastery dedicated to the Dormition of the Virgin was the most important one in the Korthi region. It had many cells arranged on two floors, ancillary spaces, and a katholikon famous for its carved cedar sanctuary screen. Its founding date is unknown. It has always housed monks. In 1818, its assets devolved to the jurisdiction of the School of the Ayia Triada Moskionas and later to the Greek School in Korthi. These events signalled its dissolution. Today one can see a relatively small, simply laid out, walled – with the obvious intention of fortification – monastery in harmony with the spare landscape. Recent conservation efforts have given it a pleasant appearance, with the blue courtyard gate and whitewashed surfaces. Outside the wall there is a flowing spring and around the monastery are well-tended chapels. This site is fairly deserted, with a beautiful view of the coast.

1

2

3

1. Convent of Ayia Eirini.
2. Convent of Ayia Marina.
3. Monastery of Tromarchia (Our Lady Tromarchiani).

Chora.

TOUR

Andros (CHORA)
pp. 60 - 85

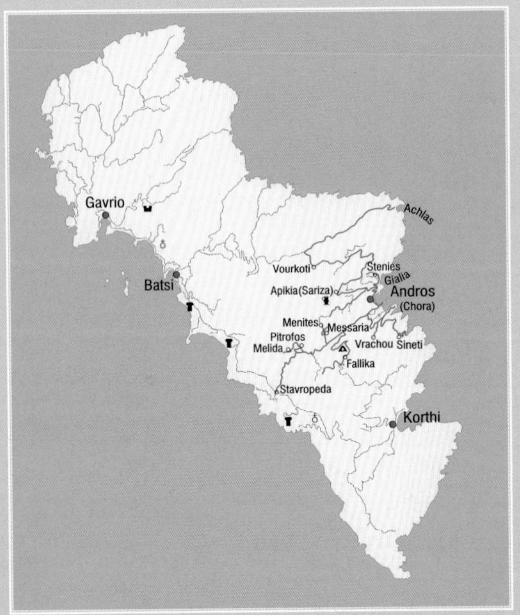

a. Presentation of Chora p. 60
b. Itineraries starting from Chora p. 75
Chora-Vourkoti p. 75
Chora-Stavropeda p. 80
Chora-Sineti-Dipotamata p. 84

GAVRIO
pp. 86 - 97

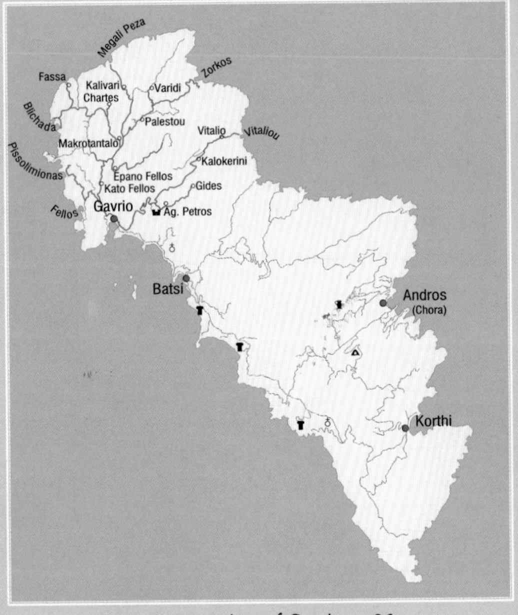

a. Presentation of Gavrio p. 86
b. Itineraries starting from Gavrio p. 92
Gavrio-Fellos-Makrotantalo region p. 92
Gavrio-Ano Ayios Petros-Vitali p. 97

Don't miss...

IN CHORA:
- *Kairios Library p. 64*
- *Church of the Dormition of the Virgin p. 65*
- *Kairi Square p. 65*
- *Goulandri Square p. 65*
- *Archaeological Museum p. 67*
- *Museum of Modern Art p. 67*
- *Chapel of Ayia Thalassini p. 69*
- *Tourlitis Lighthouse p. 69*
- *Paraporti p. 69*
- *Church of the Virgin Theoskepasti p. 69*
- *Church of Ayios Georgios p. 69*
- *Maritime Museum p. 70*
- *Residence of Theophilos Kairis p. 70*

IN GAVRIO:
- *Church of Ayios Nikolaos p. 86*
- *Liopesi p. 90*
- *Tower of Ayios Petros p. 90*
- *Chrysi Ammos (Golden Sand beach) p. 90*
- *Fellos Beach p. 92*

OF ANDROS

BATSI
pp. 98 - 103

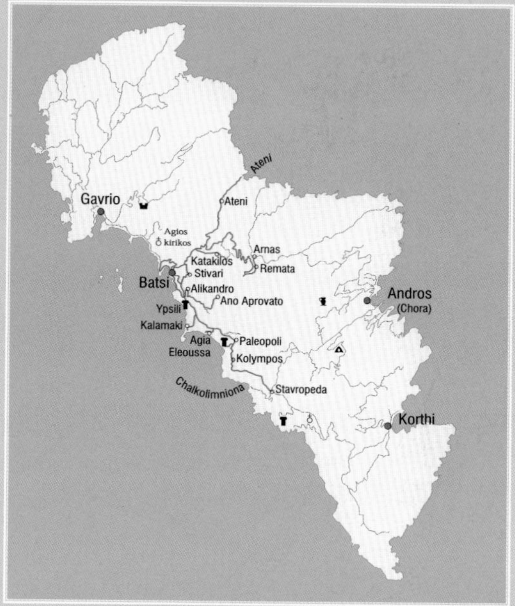

KORTHI BAY
pp. 104 - 114

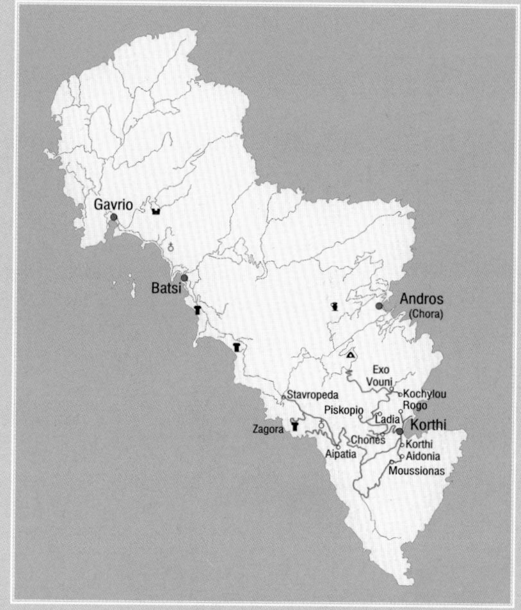

IN BATSI:
- *Church of Ayios Philipos p. 98*
- *Stivari p. 100*
- *Beach at Ateni p. 102*

IN KORTHI:
- *Kochilou p. 113*
- *The harbour of Ayia Ekaterini*
- *The beach named "The old lady's jump"*

ALSO...
- *Mountainous Arni*
- *Paleopoli and its local museum*
- *Refreshing Menites*
- *Apikia with the Sariza mineral water springs and the important monastery of Ayios Nikolaos*
- *Aidonia in the capital village of Korthi*

Andros (Chora)

The present capital of the island is the post-revolutionary form of the little fortified town of "Kastro tou Emboriou" or "Kato Kastro". It is not certain whether a Byzantine settlement existed previously on this site, but we do know that the fortifications of the older part of the city date to the period of Latin rule. The location selected on which to establish the city explains its architectural particularities. A long narrow rocky headland (390 m. long and about 200 m. at its widest spot) juts out into the sea, interrupting the calm regularity of the beaches on either side of it, which were formed

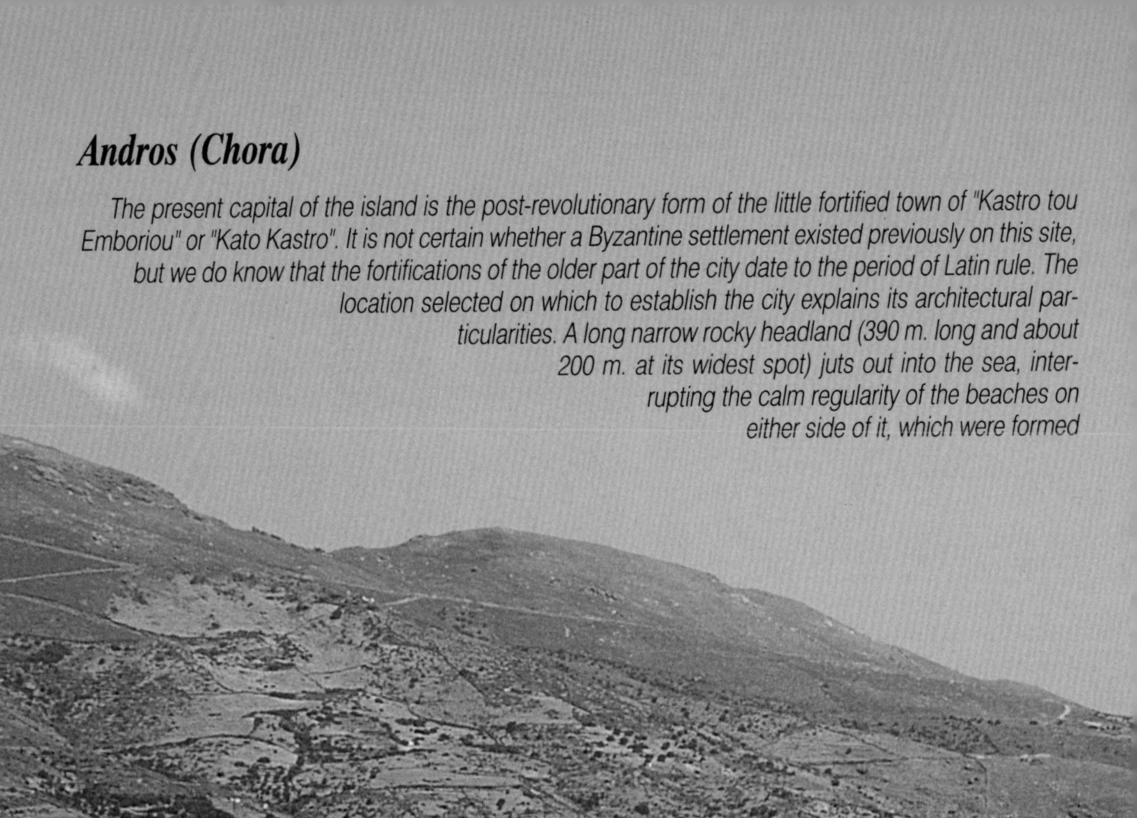

at the end of two fertile valleys. Two metres from the end of the point, a rocky islet stands in the sea as a kind of natural fortification. On this point, a fortress (Kastro) was built which was of decisive significance to the commercial interests of the Venetian lords, and to this day is connected by bridge to the tongue of land opposite.

The visitor arriving in Chora by car will first come in visual contact with its more recent sections, built on a hill between two valleys (Louria to the left and Alados to the right). The architecture here is mixed. But the visitor – who should abandon his car if he wants to enter the heart of the town - will soon be admiring the neoclassical mansions that bear witness to the prosperity of its shipowners, especially after World War I, when Chora, together with Hermopouli, claimed first place in beauty and wealth among Cycladic towns.

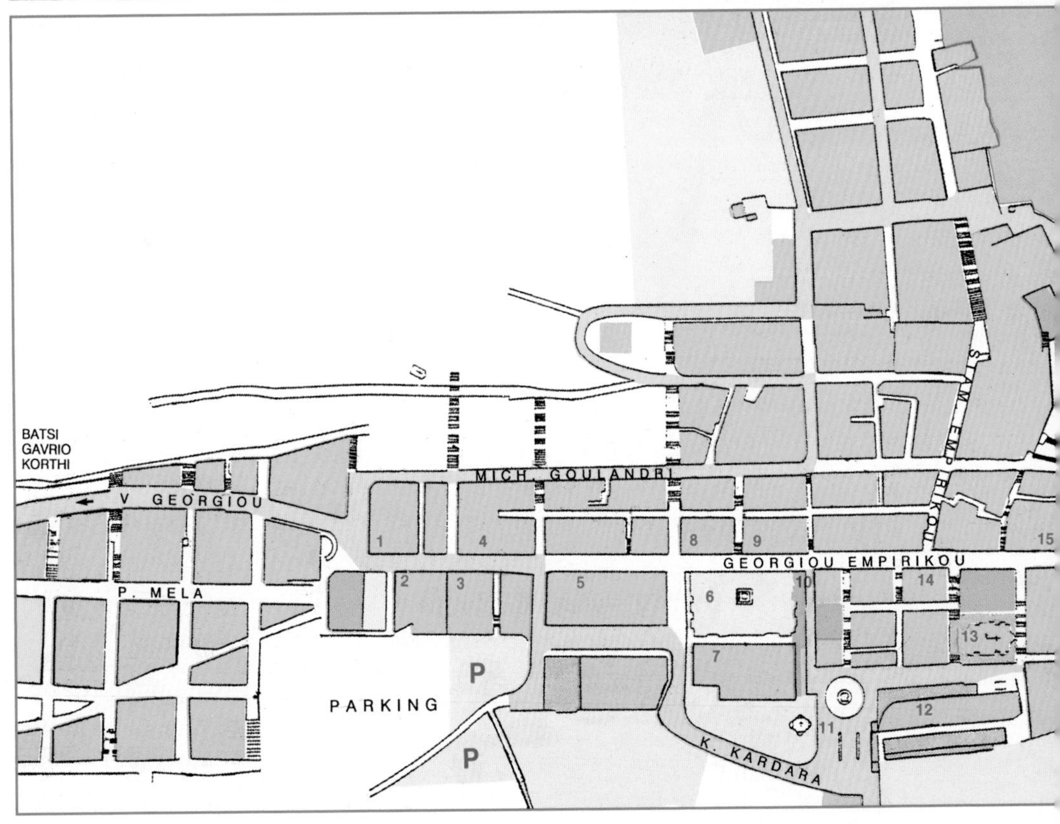
BATSI
GAVRIO
KORTHI
V. GEORGIOU
MICH. GOULANDRI
GEORGIOU EMPIRIKOU
P. MELA
PARKING
P
P
K. KARDARA
1
2
3
4
5
6
7
8
9
10
11
12
13
14
15

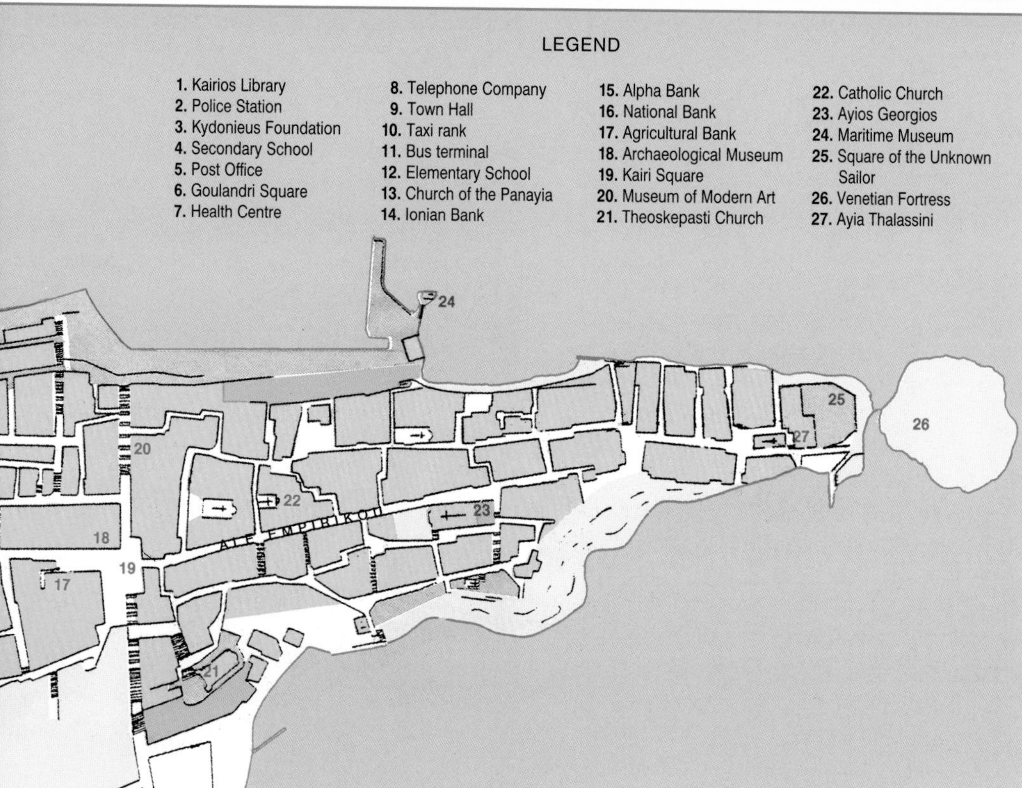
LEGEND
1. Kairios Library
2. Police Station
3. Kydonieus Foundation
4. Secondary School
5. Post Office
6. Goulandri Square
7. Health Centre
8. Telephone Company
9. Town Hall
10. Taxi rank
11. Bus terminal
12. Elementary School
13. Church of the Panayia
14. Ionian Bank
15. Alpha Bank
16. National Bank
17. Agricultural Bank
18. Archaeological Museum
19. Kairi Square
20. Museum of Modern Art
21. Theoskepasti Church
22. Catholic Church
23. Ayios Georgios
24. Maritime Museum
25. Square of the Unknown Sailor
26. Venetian Fortress
27. Ayia Thalassini

1

Characteristic examples of neoclassical buildings are the Trikoglou residence, the Voyiatzis mansion, the Drakos family building that houses the Police Station, and the elegant building which, after being donated by the Kampanis family, houses the **Kairios Library.** *Here, accommodated in a truly beautiful building, is the lending library and reading room. Some 3000 titles from the private collection of Theophilos Kairis are preserved and kept here. Visitors can also find here a wealth of information sources about Andros. Of great importance in this regard is the work of Dimitris Paschalis.*

2

Continuing in the same direction we will also find, among other things, the Empirikio Secondary School which was established in 1926 by a donation from Stamatis G. Empirikos and, virtually across the street, the home of Petros Kydonieus, which now houses the significant cultural activities (e.g. painting exhibitions) of the Foundation of the same name. Nearby is the large marble-paved V. Goulandri Square, or "Gerokomio", since the building in the archaic order that covers the south side (donated by Con. G. Empirikos) has housed the Old People's Home since 1894 and also houses the Health Centre (in one wing). The symmetry of the volumes and simplicity of forms lend grandeur to the area around the square.

3

Another magnificent building is the one we see opposite the western side of the Old People's Home. A gift of Alk. K. Empirikos, it was built in 1913 to house the Vocational School, an objective that was never fulfilled. From the eastern edge of the Gerokomio Square, we are led to the long-distance coach station, in Ayia Olga Square, beside the site on which Th. Kairis had established his school.

Continuing our walk down the stone-paved main street (Georgiou Empirikou St.)we encounter the "market" in Chora, where many of its shops are gathered, some of which retain the style of another age. Apart from its obvious commercial significance, the market is – in the ancient Greek sense of the word – the meeting place for the local people. The central point is dominated by the noble church of the Dormition of the Virgin, the most recent of the three parish churches in the town (the other two are the Theoskepasti and Ayios Georgios). It has a beautiful marble templon with gold ornamentation, a work donated by shipowner P. Goulandris. Another significant landmark in the graphic capital is the slate-paved Kairi Square on the Porta site, where the marble bust of Theophilos Kairis, philosopher and fighter for Greek independence, is located. This square inspires intimacy. Its characteristic features are the large plane tree, the marble fountain with beautiful carved ornamentation dating to 1818 – when there were very few houses in this newest section of Andros that we have seen so far – and its vaulted arcade under a house, in which is the main gate (or Porta) of the settlement of Kato Kastro.

1. Goulandri Square.
2, 3. Views of the Kairios Library.
4, 5. The great plane tree and the picturesque little coffee shops in Kairi Square are landmarks for visitors and local people alike.

1

2

1

2

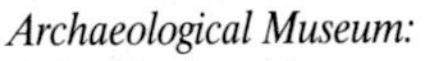

Archaeological Museum:
1. Panel of marble parapet, of unknown origin, 9th-10th century BC
2. Torso of Artemis, Roman copy dating from the 2nd century BC from Paleopoli
3. Interior of Museum.

3

*The **Andros Archaeological Museum** is situated in Kairi Square and was founded in 1981, sponsored by the Vassilios and Eliza Goulandris Foundation. A simple two-storey building in form, it includes areas on two levels for the exhibition of archaeological finds (of Theophilos Kairi, D. Paschalis and from the excavations of the Archaeological Service in Paleopoli and Zagora).*

The most impressive of the exhibits is certainly the larger-than-life figure of Hermes of Andros, a copy dating from the first century AD, reminiscent of the original by Praxiteles. It was found, together with an important statue of a woman, in Paleopoli in 1832. Findings from the Byzantine period are also exhibited.

*Thanks to the activity of the Vassilios and Eliza Goulandris Foundation, the visitor can also derive a rich visual experience from a visit to the **Museum of Modern Art** by following the stepped road beside the Archaeological Museum. The exhibition area in this museum, which was opened officially in 1979, hosts a large number of works by Michalis Tombros, flanked by examples of the work of other significant Greek artists (Tsarouchis, Gounaropoulos, Fassianos, Bouzianis, Galanis, etc.)*

Opposite is the new wing of the Museum of Modern Art, which has been open since 1986. Every summer it has become the custom to show representative works by famous artists of international repute in its fine, four-level exhibition area.

4

4. Corinthian capital from Paleopoli, 4-5th cent. BC.
5. Exhibition at the Museum of Modern Art.

5

1

The same stairs that lead to the museums end at a beautiful, typically picturesque island spot: the district of Plakoura, adorned by the wave-swept chapel of Ayia Thalassini. This lovely picture is framed by the ruins of the north side of the Venetian castle with the Tourlitis lighthouse in the background, which is also frequently lashed by waves. Opposite Plakoura is Nimbori beach and a jetty to walk on.

A path off the square leads to the beach on the other side of Chora, a large, beautiful and sandy beach called **Paraporti**. *If we make a little detour to the left on the way down, we can visit the chapel of the protectress of the entire island, the* **Virgin Theoskepasti**. *Both the discovery of an icon of the Virgin Hodeghetria (who shows the way), which is believed to be Byzantine in origin although it cannot be more precisely dated, and the completion of the church are attributed to a miracle, which was the securing of the timber required to build the roof, by means of the miraculous salvaging of a boat off the coast.*

In addition, the intensive employment of Andriots as sailors linked the worship of the Theoskepasti with the longing and worries of the seamen's families. The church owes its current form to an enlargement-renovation (in 1555) and to successive repairs. Externally, it is spare and unadorned. Its interior is ornamented with a splendid templon and many valuable votive objects.

The name Paraporti, which refers to the entire architecturally distinct district on the southern side of the old town, was taken from a small gate next to the Porta (Paraporti = beside the gate). The narrow little streets, which leave minimal space between the houses, are labyrinthine. Most of the houses built in the Venetian period have not survived. But everything is indicative of island architecture, and the visitor can easily understand its virtues, in its wise utilisation of private and public space.

A central cobbled street (Alk. Empirikou) runs through this entire graphic, historic part of the city in which, because of its fortification, most of the Frankish and Turkish families lived. At the beginning of the street (from the Porta), a narrow lane to the left leads to the Byzantine church of Palatiani, dating from the 13th century, a domed, cross-in-square church that was renovated in 1712. A little farther on is the Catholic church of Ayios Andreas (St Andrew). Also worth visiting is the church of Ayios Georgios on Empirikou St.
On its façade, there is a noteworthy marble relief of St George. Beyond the church's forecourt is the house, now closed, in which Th. Kairis was born.

Near the church is the Municipal Theatre, where events can be held in the summer and which functions as a cinema in the winter. The cobbled street continues, after curving slightly toward the Riva district. Here we can see Western influences, such as the vaulted verandas on the houses or the façade of the little church of Ayia Varvara (St Barbara). We visit the **Maritime Museum,** *whose exhibits reveal the gradual growth of Andriot shipping; we gaze at the*

2

1. The chapel of Ayia Thalassini.
2. The Tourlitis lighthouse.

old-time official Andriot dress, and then we end up with a wonderful surprise, the marble-paved Riva Square, at the tip of the peninsula of Chora, in which stands the Memorial to the Unknown Sailor, a magnificent bronze statue by Michalis Tombros, a tribute to the Andriot seaman's contribution to the island in war and peace. The site was donated to the Municipality of Andros by the Empirikos family. Its landscaping and the establishment of the Maritime Museum were funded by a donation from the sons of Nikolaos Goulandris.

From Riva Square there is a magnificent view of the fortress or Kastro and the arched bridge, which was rebuilt after a storm in 1952 using the same techniques and the old materials. Recently, the Tourlitis lighthouse, another emblem of Andros, was restored to its initial condition also through a donation. All these are particularly impressive if they are seen from the Nimbori coast opposite. The road beside the Kairios Library and the other mansions at the entrance to the town leads there. We pass through Sinikismos – the district created in 1926 in which the refugees from Asia Minor were housed – and thus we arrive at a large beach, the most social one in the region.

At one end, toward the breakwater, is

1

2

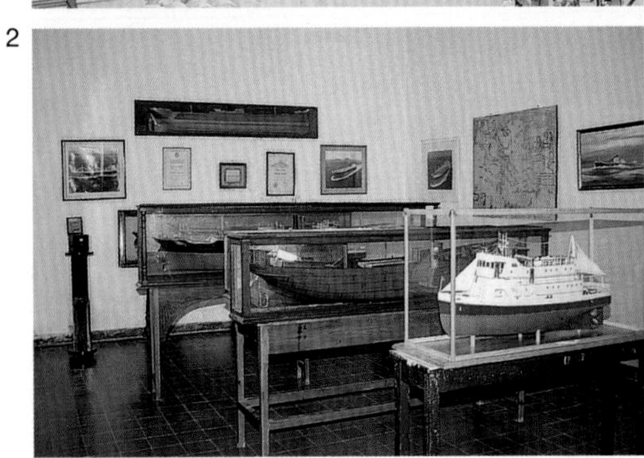

the Andros Yacht Club and opposite is the elegant church of Ayios Nikolaos.

Continuing along the coastal road, we come to the Chora harbour in where passenger ships no longer dock, although many private craft are accommodated. And finally, a visit to the cemetery of Andros, in the Pefkakia district at the western edge of the city, is also worthwhile since is it adorned by many superb sculptures, most of which are creations by Georgios D. Ramoundos from Amonakli, Korthi. The splendour of the grave monuments, as well as many of their themes constitute yet another important testimony of the prestige of Andriot shipping, and reinforce theimpression of nobility gained by walking through Chora.

1. As strange as it may seem, the Chora cemetery is one of the most interesting sights on the island, as many of its grave monuments are also significant sculptures.
2. Interior of the Maritime Museum.
3. View of Chora from the ruins of the Venetian fortress.

3

Yialia – Stenies.

1

2

Chora – Vourkoti

This tour gives us a flavour of the island's special beauty, and includes a visit to Stenies and Apikia – both famous villages – and to the northern settlements of the communities of Lamira, Ipsilou, Mesathouri, Strapouries. A visit to the Monastery of Ayios Nikolaos will be a special experience as well as to the mountainous Vourkoti. At the 1.5 km. point on the road between Chora and Nimbori, i.e. at the end of the sandy beach, we head left. The twists and turns in the road do not prevent us from enjoying the superb view. After 2.5 km, we see to the right the turnoff leading to Stenies, at the foot of a low hill that looks like a natural boundary between this district and Chora (Tripes site). At the top of the hill is the little church of the Ayia Triada (Holy Trinity). Here it is that a significant figure in Andriot shipping, Leonidas A. Empirikos, father of the poet, was laid to rest in 1950.

Proceeding down the road to Stenies, we come to a fork (at about 250 m.) The road to the left goes to Pera Banta as far as the church of Ayia Varvara. It is a pretty neighbourhood built on the rocky banks of a river whose source is at Zenio; it passes through Apikia (Pithara, Apatouria) and flows into the sea at Yialia. The stone bridge here is also very old.

Of particular interest in this region is the three-story tower of Bistis-Mouvelas now an archaeological monument. It was probably built in the 17th century, and is said to be the oldest tower still standing on the island. Near it is the private church of Ayios Georgios. At the bottom of the gully we can see the ruins of Fabrika, in which a pasta factory once operated.

The main road to Stenies leads to **Yialia** *1 km. later. Here it has been observed that the deep clear, blue-green water can eliminate the substances that become attached to keels of boats if they remain there for a few days; if they stay longer it can corrode them. At Piso Yialia, there is a large sandy beach with a gentle slope, reached by a path that sets out from Ayia Fotini, the chapel after Yialia.*

A little farther on (1.6 km), a turn to the right leads to the upper districts of the amphitheatrically built village. The main road (2.25 km) takes us to its most central points, with the gardens, the little shops, and the roofed fountain-washery (Pentavrysi).

3

1. The Yialia beach.
2. The village of Stenies.
3. The Bistis tower.

Stenies *is unquestionably a splendid example of the financial prosperity of the island's residents. A neighbouring village, famous for the Sariza springs, is* **Apikia**. *We return to the main road and drive another four km (a total of 7 km from Chora). Just before arriving in Apikia, we come upon a narrow downhill road to the right (1 km) that will take us to Apatouria, a pretty district nestled in the lower spots. As we go on, we'll see graphic chapels, the monastery of St Marina to the left, the gully on a sharp right turn, and then 500 metres to the left, an uphill paved road.*

At the beginning of the road, also to the left, is the path leading to Pithara, a gully that looks as though it had been laid out especially for picnickers, with flat, smooth rocks, little waterfalls and plane trees.

The highlight of the village is of course the Sariza spring. Its waters run from a marble-covered head-spring into a covered fountain at a central point in the village, a few steps from the level of the road. The inhabitants of the village were the first to notice that the slab over which the water ran was worn away very quickly, so they used this water for dysuria. Then its medicinal properties were discussed at a medical conference in Athens in 1882, where it was deemed effective for "renal gravel and stones in the bladder". The name **Sariza** *comes from a title of the Virgin who is venerated in one of the two parish churches in Apikia.*

The other parish of Apikia is the Dormition of the Virgin, or the Panayia Katasyrti, a name derived from the tradition according to which an older chapel remained intact on the edge of a cliff when a landslide pulled the entire region down into the gully. On the 15th of August, the dried lilies on the shrine burst into flower.

An unforgettable experience, which can be easily combined with a trip to Apikia is a visit to the monastery of Ayios Nikolaos.

We head eastward, on the extension of the road

1

2

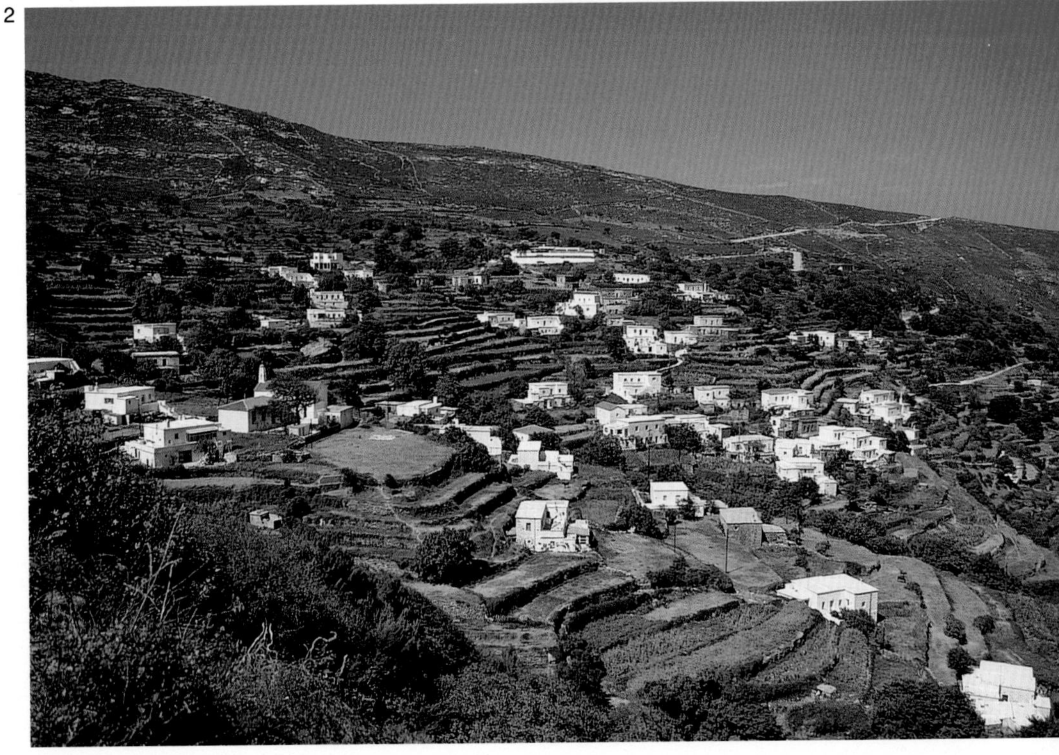

between Chora and Apikia, which becomes wider, as the landscape changes into a barer picture. Thus it is easy to discern on the right (2 km from Apikia) the convent of Ayia Eirini. We continue up the hill, and 4 km from Apikia, we meet a passable gravel road to the right, which leads to the monastery of Ayios Nikolaos Vounena. The site, Sora, is splendid, wild and isolated and the horizon is open only to the east looking out over the Achla bay. A characteristic rock bluff rises above the monastery. North of here is Katakalaii, which belongs to Apikia, and Vourkoti. Katakalaii is a very small settlement endowed with an expansive view. The paved side road after the turn off for Ayios Nikolaos leads there.

Four km along and we are in the rural village of Vourkoti (15 km from Chora). Its inhabitants still retain a good many of their customs and manners and take special pride in their summer festivals. The area is famous for its walnuts and tasty apples.

The road between Apikia and Vourkoti continues as a gravel road for another 8 km., to Arni. In the first 600 metres of this extension, i.e. on the boundaries of the settlement, another gravel road leads off to the right to the beautiful Achla beach, which with its blue-green waters, the river that brings its abundant waters to the seaside and the plane trees on its banks create a superb landscape and a significant habitat as well. But access is difficult because the 7 km. road is very steep at many points.

The return to familiar images means visiting Ipsilou, Mesathouri, Strapourgies, by taking the side road off the Chora-Apikia road. Our eyes have become accustomed to seeing trees, fountains, grand old houses, and a panoramic view. But here there are also Byzantine churches and other sights to see.

1. Apikia.
2., 4. Vourkoti.
3. The beach at Achla.

After the first 500 metres on this road, we can see the sign (right) indicating a good gravel road that will take us to the monastery of Ayia Marina after 2 km. Continuing along the paved road, another 600 metres on, there is a side road to the left leading to **Kato Ipsilou**, where we find the Byzantine church of the **Taxiarchis** (Archangel), a domed church of the two-columned inscribed cross type. Its foundation dates to the late 11th century; we can see that here too interventions have altered its initial form. The decorative members of the exterior surface may be from the period of Latin rule.

Another 1.5 km down the road, the stop for Ipsilou is located at a particularly sharp curve.

The Dormition of the Virgin in Mesathouri is a significant Byzantine church. One km. along the main paved road from Ipsilou and just a few metres from the lefthand turn for Mesathouri (we soon see the little church of Ayios Georgios) we will find the Church of the Dormition, which is another domed church of the inscribed cross type, and dates to the late 12th-early 13th century. It has sustained several unfortunate changes, but its plasticity nevertheless remains impressive, culminating in the double-vaulted octagonal dome.

The settlement right after Mesathouri is **Strapouries**, which extends almost to the top of the deeply shaded hill. The first thing to draw our attention is the stone chapel of Ayios Nikolaos on the road. Beyond it is the parish church of Ayios Panteleimon, of a newer order, and behind it the little 25th of March Square. From here on, it is worth going on foot to the higher parts of the village, with its picturesque Valaha fountain, the rock of Gremnistra and the chapel of the Prophet Elijah at the highest point, from which is a stunning view. Gremnistra is a vertical cave-like rock the surface of which is usually damp from water seepage. At the foot of the rock, seats have been built for people to rest on.
The little church of Ayios Yiannis Nisteftis (St John the Faster), the so-called Kamarianos, is an attractive structure. It is below the road, at

1

2

about the level of Ayios Panteleimon, beside the old cemetery. Its main features are the solid arcade and benches in the cloister, surrounding it like stone lace, a fact that lends the modest little church an unexpected dignity.

The walk from this point on, down the cobbled street, holds another surprise: The tower of Athinaios. It is a real mansion, a luxury residence with Western-style ornamental features on its façade and plasticity reminiscent of nothing we have seen so far of Andriot architecture.

We have just about arrived at the western end of the settlement. From here the road leads to Ano Menites. Along the way, we encounter the Meliti spring with its excellent drinking water. It is easily recognisable from the stone structures around it (dovecote, huts, cistern, benches around the plane trees), elements that combine to create a beautiful picture.

1. The church of Ayios Taxiarchis.
2. Views of Ipsilou.

1

Chora – Stavropeda

Starting off from the intersection beside the Kairios Library and heading ever westward, we come to a representative area which, based on geographical, historicaland social criteria, is part of the Chora region.

Before we have covered even one km on the provincial road, we can see the settlements of Livadia, Vrachnou and Lamira in a verdant setting. At the 5 km point, an attractive prospect opens out: to turn left and drive the 2.5 km of the road around Mesaria. It is a very pleasant drive, owing to the privileged view it provides of the fertile valley of the Klados stream. A magnificent building can be glimpsed through the greenery: it is the well-preserved mansion of Sp. Zaphiropoulos, built in 1839.

1. The church of Ayios Nikolaos.
2. Mesaria.
3. The bridge at Aladinos.

2

However, to become better acquainted with the graphic and historical village of Mesaria, we stay on the main road, which soon narrows considerably. At this point (2.1 km) we can see a side road to the right and from there a narrow paved road (1 km) leads to the main settlement of Lamira. The landscape, an attractive synthesis of space and buildings – most of which bear witness to wealth and gentility – is idyllic. The lowest level is a fertile valley created by the Louria river. On the slopes, up to the northernmost settlements of Strapouries, Mesathouri, and Ipsilou, the vegetation is lush. One of the most worthwhile ecclesiastical monuments in the main settlement of Mesaria is the parish church of **Ayios Nikolaos**, and the important Byzantine church of the Taxiarchis (Archangel), a domed, two-columned church of the 12th century. One is impressed by its lovely proportions, the well-preserved external form of its walls and its decorative details.

A few metres beyond, on the left side of the road, stands another remarkable monument, this time of a secular nature, the Tower of Lorenzo Kairis, one of the most recent to be saved, dating from 1760.

Along the 3.5-km route, we see the end of the regional road to the left. From this point precisely, we abandon the provincial road once again, and head for the Pera Horia and the monastery of Panachrantos (St Panteleimon).

After the first few kilometres on this narrow paved road of this particular route, a side road to the right leads to the stop at **Aladino**, with a pretty cluster of houses around the church of Ayia Triada (Holy Trinity).

Continuing on, 1.5 km. later, we arrive in an attractive place, with a large bridge in the shadow of high trees and with elegant homes around it. A little farther on, a stone-paved road starts out that leads to the cave area, which has already begun to be developed. Back to the asphalt road, and we ascend to a point (3.3. km) where the paved road to the left leads to Fallika, a settlement with an unrestricted view to the east, built right below the monastery. If we pass this side road, we are heading west and reach the end of the paved road, having come to

3

Koureli (3.8 km, where we'll find a left-hand turn off, not the most advisable, for the monastery) and Sasa (4.8 km). The few houses of Alado are located on the extension of this route.

1. The cave of Aladino.
2. Traditional house in Aladino.
3. The village of Pitrofos.
4. Fountains in Menites.

1

2

3

The next stop is the lush green, cool village of **Menites**. *The provincial road across Mesaria, after 4.3 km, meets the turn-off to the right for Menites where the beauty of the landscape is unforgettable, as well-tended homes, mansions, dovecotes and other buildings can be seen on different levels among the orchards.*

The most typical point, at the end of the side road is where the village fountains are found, below the church of the Virgin of Koumoulou – from which the spring of the same name bubbles up – in the shade of ancient trees. Many have identified this site with the centre of the ancient Dionysiac cult famous in Andros where, according to tradition, the spring that bubbled up in the sanctuary of Dionysus would give forth wine during the days of his festival.

An alternative possibility for admiring the site is offered by the turn off (to the left) for Ano Menites, from which you can enjoy a view of the entire settlement, as well as the broader region we have seen so far.

Pitrofos *is a village on the way to Stavropeda (10.8 km from Chora). A characteristic scene is the shady square beautifully framed by houses and churches among which the parish church of Ayios Panteleimon stands out. For nature lovers, a hike in the hills is recommended.*

As we proceed northwards, we see the few houses of **Melida** *in a green setting, with an inaccessible gully, while the end of the local road is reached at the 7.8 km point.*

One familiar, serene picture of the Andriot countryside succeeds another, as we follow the curves in the asphalt road, and only the view of another stark white Byzantine church prepares us for a change of scene. It is the Taxiarchis (Archangel) of Melida, a domed inscribed-cross church very likely built in the second half of the 11th century, which retains its elegance despite subsequent changes (the exterior was plastered over and the Byzantine terracotta roof tiles were replaced with slate). It once had a splendid marble chancel screen which, in the 18th century, was used to decorate the façade of the church of Ayios Nikolaos in Mesaria.

4

1

Chora – Sineti – Dipotamata

This tour completes the fairly full picture we have already formed of the settlements that flank the island's capital. The point of departure is still the intersection near the Kairios Library. From there, we head toward the western exit of Chora and at 0.8 km, we can see the road to Korthi on the left.

At the point where this road encounters the Alado stream on the left, a narrow concrete road (2 km) leads to the fertile plane and the Paraporti beach, where the municipal athletic facilities are located. Then, heading now upward, we pass through the middle of **Livadia**, dominated by the church of Ayios Konstantinos.

Here our gaze is drawn by the outermost houses of Vrachnou. A paved road (1 km) leads to this densely inhabited village with the famous view, starting from the right-hand turn off (at 3.65 km). Two hundred metres along (to the left) is the road to the monastery and the heliport.

As far as Sineti, the road follows the folds in the coastline that create the little inlets of Volia and Lidi.
At 7 km, we reach the point where the left-hand turn will reveal what it would be impossible to imagine if we'd stayed on the main road: a dense cluster of houses, many trees and all those features that make up a typical Andriot village. It is **Sineti**, the southernmost village in the group of some 20 settlements that surrounds Chora.

It is worth noting that according to the recent administrative division of the island, Sineti and Dipotamata belong to the municipality of Korthi. Sineti is laid out on a steep slope that ends in a gully, with Dipotamata running almost to the sea. A paved road leads to the beach, which is the pride of the inhabitants.

The inaccessible, narrow valley attracts travellers, as well as specialist scholars, as a habitat, and thanks to its 22 water mills that have been preserved to date. Access is possible on a gravel road at 9 km. For pedestrians, the well preserved cobbled street that links Vouni, Kochilou and the other villages of the Apano Dimos and Chora, and will also serve the use of the water mills, is expected to be restored.

The entire Dipotamata region up to Vouni and Kochilou, is like a gorge.

1. The Livadia plane.
2. Sineti.

2

Gavrio

The first image of the island of Andros seen by the visitor travelling on a ship of the line is Gavrio, a coastal town with a sheltered port (maximum security) and many shops and services (port authority, banks, travel agents, telephones, post office, etc.). The original settlement was built in accordance with an urban plan during the reign of Otho (mid-19th century). Today Gavrio occupies a large area from the Ayii Saranta hills (where the hamlets of Koumari, Xirokampos, and Ano Gavrio are located) and down to the beach – one of the most densely populated areas – and the districts of Ayios Petros and Kypri that are being developed. The main settlement is simple and picturesque, virtues that are strongly evident when traffic in the port calms down and one can hear only the sound of the fishing boats coming and going. From the ship's deck you can see the lighthouse, inextricably linked with feelings of waiting and separation, the parish church of Ayios Nikolaos in the most conspicuous place, and beyond, the convent of Zoodochos Piyi (Ayias), against the background of Petalo.

Gavrio.

1

In Gavrio there is a camping site, as well as hotels and other tourist accommodation along the road to Batsi, and all along the coat. The island's main road, which starts right opposite the point where the ships dock and the passengers disembark, runs along the coast. As we head toward Batsi, we come first to the cove named ***Liopesi****. Right afterwards we can see the vast sandy beach of* ***Ayios Petros*** *in the shade of the village of the same name and of its tower. Just a few metres separate this beach from the next one,* ***Psili (or Chrisi) Ammos*** *(Fine or Golden Sand) where the clean, brilliant white beach absolutely justifies its name. Farther along we come to* ***Kypri*** *with its beach of the same name; these are the traditional southern boundaries of the Gavrio region.*

1, 2. The tower and fountain of Ayios Petros.
3. Chrysi Ammos.

2

3

Gavrio – Fellos – Makrotantalos region

To get better acquainted with the northern section of the island, we head in the opposite direction, on the road that took us to southeastern Andros, initially along the quay and plain of Gavrio. A paved road brings us to a point opposite the town where (1.8 km) to our left is Charakas, a growing residential site with a beautiful view of the harbour. Continuing on the paved road, we find ourselves (3 km) at the junction for Kato Fellos and its coast (to the left) and for Ano Fellos and the Makrotantalo region to the right. We head left and note some typical examples of the architectural tradition. An asphalt side road to the right (at 900 metres) leads to most of the well-kept houses of Kato Fellos. The next side road to the right (4.5 km from Gavrio), after 4 km of gravel road across the Fellos plain and through the hills, invites us to visit the magic ***Pisolimniona****, on the remote western coast with its gently sloping terrain and crystal waters.*

The long sandy beach of ***Fellos*** *(5.5. km) is flanked by low hills and country homes. Here the water deepens gradually. From its left side, a gravel road leads (after 1.3 km) to Kourtali, an inlet with fine sand.*

The remaining itinerary includes the villages of Makrotantalo, to which we are heading, having come back to the first crossroads (3 km from Gavrio). We pass through Pano Fellos with its splendid view. The landscape is spare and soft. Many signs testify to the existence among the hills of sparsely populated rural settlements. At 3.3 km (from the intersection) a side road to the left leads to Chartes, Nermingies, and Fassa, the promontory on the north coast of the island, on top of which (212 metres) there is a stone lighthouse of great luminosity.

At 4.3 km to the right, is a gravel road leading to historic Amolochos. Five kilometres later, after a fairly easy ascent on a wide gravel road, one arrives at the village the greater part of which has been abandoned. Nevertheless the location, with important vestiges of its vernacular architecture, at least what can be discerned through the vegetation, is sufficient to justify a visit. The fountain of Mouria is lovely, with water of the highest quality. Lower down, in the settlement Frousaii, large farm complexes with water mills have been preserved, proving it to have been a mill village. The most impressive structures in the region of Amolochos are the church of the Panayia, believed to be Byzantine, which belonged to the Dimitriou family, and the ***tower of Giannoulis Dimitriou****, built in 1815.*

1

2

1. The tower of Giannoulis Dimitriou.
2. The lighthouse of Fassa.
3. The Fellos beach.
4. Pisolimnionas.

3

4

Returning to the main paved road at the 5.5 km point (from the Fellos intersection), another sideroad to the left leads to Chartes and Sidonta. Generally speaking, many passable gravel roads have been built in the region and if visitors want to go to Fassa or some other point on the northwest coast (Makrotantalo tower, Ayios Sostis, etc.) they should have a lot of time and interest at their disposal.

At 6 km. there's a fork in the paved road. The road to the right evolves into a passable, wide gravel road, which serves the sparsely populated regions of Palestos (= wrestler, place name in memory of the Andriot Olympic victor Ieronymos), Daphnia, Kapsala and the rich valley of Varidi with a stream that stems from Frousaii and ends on the eastern coast. On the slope to the left, the towers of a **wind farm** are visible, as are Kalivari and Ano Varidi (to which the left hand, ascending branch of the road goes). Continuing on, firmly oriented eastwards, we end up in the delightful, almost exotic location of **Zorkos** bay (16.8 km from Gavrio). The force of the waves in winter creates terraces with sand and pebbles on the large, broad coast. The sea floor drops off after just a few steps and can only be seen with difficulty. This place requires strong, skilled swimmers. The bare landscape is relentless, its bond with the sea captivating.

On the way back, if we go through Kalivari, we will see a sign showing the way to Peza bay in the middle of the island's north coast. To be precise, we are talking here about "twin" northern bays, Mikri (small) and Megali (large) Peza, isolated, beautiful, inaccessible, and hospitable only when there is no wind. On the way back, after taking the right side road up a little hill, we can see the Tower by the sea and then the long beach of **Blihada**.

1

2

3

1. Zorkos. 2. Peza. 3. Blichada.
4. Wind farm.
5. Fountain at Mouria (Amolochos).

4

5

1

2

Gavrio – Ano Ayios Petros – Vitali

Starting out from the port of Gavrio, on the Gavrio-Chora road, we come to a road to the left. After 200 metres along this road, we head to the right (the left branch belongs to the local Gavrio road), up a narrow ascending paved road that leads to **Ano Ayios Petros** *along a route with a fantastic view. At the 2.7 km point, we can see to the right the shortest of the gravel roads leading to the tower, although the safest access to the monument is on foot. Opposite the tower, traces of the old mines are visible. Farther north, we can see the settlement's houses through the trees, old and new houses that blend in with the landscape. At 5 km, a road to the right leads to the village "stop" with the picturesque church of Ayios Petros.*

Continuing on the road to Vitali, at 5.5 km, a side road to the right leads to the settlement of **Yides**. *As we head east, we cross a deserted region. At one point along the way, the chapel of Ayia Marina appears with plane trees in its little churchyard, and beyond, an unexpected and moving image, the ruins of the monastery of the Pantokratoras (or Sotiros) of Yides, of which only the main church (katholikon) has been preserved. It was founded in the Kamariza region by the monk Maximos Magnentios or Moses, in 1596, while the katholikon, a good-sized, elaborate cross-in-square church was completed in 1613. It had two domes, cloisters, and marble columns. But the ground was too soft to support a structure of this weight, and it rapidly suffered serious damage. Thus the effort to repair it (late 18th century) offered only temporary results. Meanwhile, in 1634, the monastery was incorporated into the Ayias Monastery.*

After 9.2 km we reach **Kalokerini**, *a settlement near a gully, with cypress and olive trees, well-tended dry stone retaining walls and typical rural houses. Continuing on from this point, on a gravel road, we see the* **Vitali** *valley. A large number of side roads lead to various points in the valley, usually to houses. We head toward the sea, following a road parallel to the bed of a little stream that runs through Vitali and empties into the bay at a beach which absolutely justifies the 15 km we have already driven. A broad beach with sand and pebbles, sparkling deep waters, blue-green near the shore and dark blue in the deep waters, with a little stone chapel, a modest jewel of the beach, and with a view of the island's eastern shores. To the right, behind the rocks a similar bay (Yides) is formed on the spot where the gravel road ends.*

1. The view from Ayios Petros.
2, 4. The beach at Vitali and a church in the village.
3. The Yides beach.

3

4

Batsi

Batsi was the first part of the island to be developed for tourism. Its geographical position, its unique view of the bay with the little port (for caiques or leisure craft) and the long sandy beach (Lykeio), the amphitheatrical arrangement of the initial settlement with the church of **Ayios Philippos**, the blue lines of the horizon and the brushstrokes of green all together make a picture that one would be more likely to find in a painting. Apart from the landscape, the visitor is impressed by the mild climate, the facilities for swimming, sea sports, the boat trips around the nearby beaches, fishing, and nightlife. All around the town there are shops and accommodation for tourists. There are also banks, a post office and other services.

The picturesque village and its geographical location contributed to tourist development in Batsi.

4 ΑΔΕΛΦΙΑ Ν.Ν.95

In addition to the Batsi beach, there are two other areas suitable for swimming, and the road from the Iroon monument leads to them: **Stivari** (pebbles, rocks and deep water) and Delevoya (sandy, flat terrain) at the mouth of a gully. From there, a gravel road a few metres long takes us to the graphic bay of Ayia Marina (Aprovatou region) with the chapel of the same name at the bottom of a green gully. Throughout this entire region, you will see memorable sunsets.

Returning to the Iroon and going 600 metres beyond it, we come to a second intersection where the regional road ends on the left (2.5 km). This same road to our right continues on to Chora, Korthi and the villages in between.

Batsi to the Zoodochos Piyi (Ayias) Convent

Just a few kilometres separate Batsi from Gavrio. Between the two is Xilokarida which, with a beautiful view of the sea and the Gavrionisia, is a good destination for a hike, as well as for swimming in the little inlets along the way. In fact, just two kilometres from the point at which the extension of the coastal road from Batsi meets the provincial road to Gavrio, one arrives at a point which offers two interesting possibilities: to the right is an upward 4-km road to the convent of Zoodochos Piyi and to the left is rest or swimming in the cove of Ayios Kyprianos with the graphic little church of the same name on the shore.

1. Panoramic view of Batsi.
2. The beach at Batsi.

3. The Ayios Kyprianos cove with its chapel.
4. Stivari.

1

2

3

4

Batsi – Katakilos – Ateni – Arni

Long before Batsi was systematically inhabited, the settlements of Katakilos and Arni had been established on favourable sites, from the point of view of a water supply and natural protection. In fact, according to the Philippidis-Konstantas "New Geography" of 1791, Arni was the largest village on Andros. The region is popular today in summer months because of its cool climate, its cheerful and hospitable inhabitants, its delicious natural products and eastern beaches, which are gradually being "discovered". Also well known are its religious feasts held with devout consistency especially during the summer months (17/7, 27/7, 15/8, 23/8, 28/8 etc.).

A paved road starts from the local Batsi road at just about the point at which we meet the church of Ayios Philippos, and ascends for 2.6 km up to the intersection, where it then heads downhill into Katakilos. At 3.8 km, a narrower paved road on the left leads to the settlement of Ateni. The chapel of Ayios Panteleimon is the most noteworthy of all the chapels in the region because the local people celebrate its feast day every summer in the traditional way. A few metres down the road, and to the right, a path can barely be discerned that leads to the ruins of the old monastery of Ayios Athanasios (or the Moni Lavras or Ayia Moni). It was at its most active before 1581 when it was dissolved. The ruins one can see today give just some small impression of its former greatness. Many of its marble members have been used to build the parish church of Ayios Ioannis Theologos (St John the Divine).

The paved road to Ateni continues along a narrow valley. At one point it becomes a gravel road as the valley widens and becomes a fertile plain, and the sight of a long beach with white sand welcomes us. A small headland, on which stands a little monastery church, separates the large beach from the smaller and more popular one on the left. Thus, the smaller beach is more appropriate for safe swimming in the shallow waters or for playing on the flat sandy beach, while the larger one, which is exposed to the northeasterly winds, is ideal for sea sports.

The main settlement of Katakilos, sparsely

1

populated, is arranged around the ravine. It is divided into Kato (Lower) and Ano (Upper) Katakilos. A central point in Kato Katakilos (4.3 km) is the "square" in the ravine. Off the main paved road to the right is a side road going up to Ano Katakilos, where the parish church of Ayios Ioannis Theologos is located. Continuing on, we head toward the next stop which is worth seeing, the Arni region.

After a succession of tight curves, we come to the lush green **Remata** region. It is worth going from one end of the ravine to the other to see its ancient trees, abundant waters, the waterfall, the ruined mills and the architecturally genuine farmhouses of the settlement. The area is dominated by the church of the Evangelistria, well-kept thanks mainly to donations from Greeks abroad. The little chapel of Ayia Kyriaki is a graphic site, and tradition says that it was once used as a secret school during the years of Turkish rule.

From the Evangelistria, we climb up the slope on which the districts of **Arni** are situated, a road that becomes very difficult in winter. Here, even in summer, the air is cool, thanks to the clouds and ancient trees. The pace of life of the inhabitants, who are farmers, retired seamen or repatriated Greeks from abroad – is calm, but in summer the many visitors include Arniots living in Athens or abroad and other travellers, and the pace quickens perceptibly. The local feast days are celebrated with great enthusiasm, mainly the feast of the Saviour (6 August) and the Virgin Mary (15 August).

Just before arriving in Arni we can see towering over the village, almost suspended, a rocky headland on which is the chapel of the Prophet Elijah, in which the monk Christophoros Papoulakos preached, after being closed in a cell at the Panachrantos monastery, and exerted a major influence on the ethos of the town's inhabitants. With the appropriate vehicle, one can combine this visit with a swim at Lefka or Vori (that you have to take difficult gravel roads to get to) or head toward Vourkoti, another village on Petalo.

1. The falls at Remata.
2. The beach at Ateni and the church of the Ayia Moni.
3. Fountain at Katakilo.

2

3

Batsi.

Batsi – Stavropeda

All the sights on this particular itinerary are situated along the provincial road. Distances are measured from the point at which the extension of the coast road meets the provincial road to Stavropeda.

***Aprovato(u)**, the first village after Batsi, offers one of the most beautiful views on the island from any point in its large area. We pass through Alikandro, Koutsi and Kalamaki in turn. Heading left from Koutsi (2.4 km), a paved road leads up to the highest points on this slope of Petalo, where the houses of Kato and Ano Aprovato and its many little churches are scattered among the orchards, hidden behind their flowered courtyards. At Koutsi, to the right of the main road, is the archaeological site of Ipsili. Within a fenced area, a significant settlement from the Geometric period is being excavated, similar to that of Zagora. The citadel was surrounded by a fortified wall; the foundations of a temple and of other buildings have been found in good condition. It is estimated that the site was inhabited in the 9th century BC. Access to the leeward beaches of Prasini Ammos and Koutsi is easy only from the sea (e.g. from Batsi).*

*Continuing along our way under the strict gaze of the Kouvara massif, we come (6.1 km) to a turnoff to the right for the settlement of Ayia Eleousa Paleopoli. At 7 km we find the main settlement of **Paleopoli**, one of the most beautiful villages, if a comparison can be made, built on a steep, verdant slope – with cliffs at the highest points, and with visible little waterfalls – which leads down into the valley and onto the open beach. Since this village spreads out on both sides of the road, side roads to the left and right lead to the districts of Ano and Kato Paleopoli. Unforgettable images will remain from a stroll through the narrow lanes of the village.*

At a central point is the Archaeological Museum (open every Wednesday morning) that houses many of the findings from the region. Noteworthy among them are a larger-than-life lion taken from the "southern cemetery", a Roman sarcophagus of granite (entire, with 1/3 of its cover), the only complete hymn to Isis that has been found in Greece, and Roman inscriptions. The museum can also provide recommendations of the most archaeologically interesting sites on the island.

The road opposite the museum leads fairly close to the long beach, where swimming is very pleasant as long as the wind isn't blowing. At 9.5 km, located in a craggy area, is Kolimbos Paleopoli. From here on, the landscape becomes wilder, with ever sparser vegetation and buildings (e.g. the chapel of Ayia Thekla), an impression we retain until Stavropeda (13.5 km), where the island's main intersection can be found.

The road to the left leads to Chora, and

the road to the right to Korthi. Apart from these two immediately visible directions, the first right, a smaller side road, leads to the isolated beach of ***Chalkolimniona*** *(2.5 km).*

1. The beach at Chalkolimniona.
2. Paleopoli.

Korthi Bay

Korthi Bay, or Yialos as its inhabitants prefer to call it, or Korthi alone for the rest of Andros, was the shipbuilding centre of the region.

Serving ships heading to Istanbul and Smyrna, it evolved into a local commercial and industrial centre. Assisting even more in this regard was the coastal shipping connection with Piraeus, Tinos and Syros. Thus the most active of the region's inhabitants gathered here, making it the focal point of life for the others. The visitor will find an organised settlement that features a unique view of most of the surrounding villages. In the square, on the sidewalk of the market (agora), on the church and on the school, we can see the imprint of the inhabitants' taste and care. The large beach is ideal for swimming as is the protected cove of Ayia Ekaterini. From there it is just a few minutes' walk behind the hill to the famous beach named Pidima tis grias (Old lady's jump). A large upright rock standing in the shallow waters justly provoked the imagination of the people. Thus the tale emerged that an old lady told some invaders about the underground path leading into the castle and later out of remorse threw herself into the sea, where her body was petrified. Some people believe that such an underground path exists. The paved road becomes gravel as it leads to Exo Rogo. Indications are that we are crossing the bed of a stream, where we turn right and in 1.5 km. we reach the lovely settlement, right at the church of the Panayia, with its famous chancel screen.

1

Korthi Bay, Korthi region

The nickname "Upper Town" which is given to the Korthi region, includes the former communities of Paleokastro, Kochilou, Ormos, Korthi (the most historic) and Kaparia. After Zaganiari, which today belongs to the Municipality of Andros, we will be reminded, from all viewpoints, of a Korthian village. The point of reference for the mileage indications will be the crossroads at the beginning of the coastal road to Ormos.

A special tour is indicated for the villages of the former community of Korthi (Aidonia, Korthi, sometimes called Ano Korthi, Moskionas, Amonakli, and Piso Meria) which is at the foot of Rachi, in a green region.

At the 0.7 km. point of **Stavropeda** *road, where the ruins of the Koumelis mansion stand, we meet a sideroad to the left that will take us to what is perhaps the most typical village, Aidonia. Given that* **Aidonia**, *as well as Korthi and Amonakli, were the leading villages of the Apano Dimos (upper town), we should not be surprised*

2

by the proud style of most of its buildings with their solid volumes and austere appearance. They extend into the region that starts out from the plain – where one finds Komi with the Theoskepasti chapel and its carved wood chancel screen – and ends in a bare rocky height rising over the last houses. Scattered through the village are significant ecclesiastical monuments such as the church of the Agii Pantes (All Saints) famous for its oak carvings, the chapel of the Ayii Saranta with sculpted marble decorations on the floor and exterior, and Ayios Panteleimon, a tiny church with a carved marble chancel screen, a wooden gynaikonitis *(women's gallery) and arches.*

At Aidonia we will see what is perhaps the most beautiful fountain in the island, called Trikrouni, with a vaulted roof, and splendid marble decorations with foliate motifs.

We then pass through Korthi, which extends from the level of the road to low down on the plain (2.5 km). A settlement next to it is Moskionas *(3 km). First we can see the church of* **Ayia Triada** *(Holy Trinity) on our right, in which the school of the same name operated. Farther on, to the left, we see a lovely complex of mainly abandoned stone houses that reveal the high level of the stonemason's craft. Opposite and to the right is Amonakli (4 km), where vessels from the Geometric period have been found. The church of the Taxiarchis is post-Byzantine.*

And finally we come to Piso Meria, *which occupies a large area. The Moustakio School, a donation by the local benefactor Petros Moustakas, is in a prominent position. It opened in 1931 and today houses the Elementary School and the Vocational School.*

The road on this special detour joins up with the main road (Ormos-Stavropeda) at the village Aipatia (4 km).

1. Fountain in Korthi.
2, 4. The village of Aidonia.
3. The church of Ayia Triada.

Korthi Bay – Exo Vouni

To get better acquainted with the picturesque villages of this region, we will need to explore two different directions: we can keep heading east toward Chora or we can turn west and head up toward Stavropeda.

The first route will show us the settlements on the slope of Gerakonas. At 2.1 km there is a road to the right that will take us to the Rogo site. At 0.4 km the road leads to one of its districts, Vorina, from which one can walk to Mesa Rogo, which is low in the ravine, and Exo Rogo opposite.

Ascending, we leave behind the landscape that includes the plain, the sea, Yialos and the villages of Rachi. At 2.3 km, at the beginning of a left turnoff, we encounter the settlement of Ano Chones, as well as Kato Chones, which is lower, truly nestled into the landscape. There is a splendid church of the Virgin built in the Byzantine style. The same turnoff continues to Ayia Marina, a settlement with a church of the same name, and Alamania (1.7 km) which runs into the beginning of the Korthi plain and its abundant olive and almond trees. Three km along the main road, we reach Piskopio, another green village with the visible features of vernacular architecture.

To the north, at 5.8 km. we come to the turn off to the right (7.5 km) for **Lardia***, yet another picturesque settlement with dovecotes, stately mansions, a pretty church (of the Saviour), and a view of the Bay. We have been observing the stately shade of the church that is the symbol of the region: Panayia Agridiotissa. It is in Giannisaio, but outside the settlement so that it can be easily seen from all sides. Tradition says that the Giannisaiots gathered together the materials and tools to build the church inside the village, but oddly enough, every day they would find them elsewhere, on the Agridia site. In the belief that the Virgin was thus expressing her wishes, they built the church on what is finally the most appropriate site.*

We meet the turnoff for Giannisaio at 6.6 km. About 0.8 km from there, precisely at the Agriodiotissa church, a path leads down to Kato Horio, in a lush setting, and the paved road to Pano Horio, known for its panoramic

1

view. Continuing on our main route, we soon see what is perhaps the loveliest spot on the route: the beautiful village of ***Kochilou*** *built on the mountain slopes, and looking over its roofs, one has a view of the limestone outcropping on which are the ruins of the Apano Kastro. It is also called Kochiliano or Faneromeni, owing to the chapel (Dormition of the Virgin) that rises out of the ruins. At Kochilou, a turnoff leads to the right at 8.2 km. At the beginning of this road, to the left, there is a passable gravel road leading to the Kastro, at the end of which there are some stairs hewn out of the rock. We recommend that you climb up those stairs.*

2

1. The village of Lardia.
2, 3. Views from the Kochilou region and the ruins of the castle.

3

1

2

Soon, we reach the point (8.7 km) where the horizon starts to narrow. (There to the left is the end of the detour gravel road from Zaganiari). We are nearing the end of this trip, at the beginning of the narrow valley through which flows the Dipotamata. All we have left to visit is ***Vouni****.*

Although we can already see Exo Vouni opposite, we encounter at 9.9. km to the left a paved road to Mesa Vouni and the Panachrantos Monastery. At 1.6 km. from there, a gravel road leads to the right and then forks. The right fork ends at the famous spring of Petrenia, with water that is particularly effective in treating kidney stones. Beside the fountain is the chapel of the same name. The left fork passes through Pano Horio, and ends at the monastery. The road is wide and generally passable, but toward the end it becomes very steep.

Mesa Vouni (1.8 km) is isolated from the surrounding settlements, solitary in a landscape that looks like a mountain plateau. The monument of the region, on a deserted site, is the Byzantine cross-vaulted church of Ayios Antonios, dating from 1141 AD. It was once the katholikon of a convent that was in operation up to 1659.

The necessary subsequent repairs etc. have not affected the magnificence of the monument. Up to Exo Vouni, the total distance from Korthi is 10.3 km.

Korthi Bay – Stavropeda

In the first 4 kms, one sees farmhouses scattered across the plain, traditional and modern farm installations (threshing floors, wells, dovecotes, greenhouses, etc.). At the same time, to the left is a revealing sight, while other points of access lead to a creek with a little bridge over it. From there we can head for a small square in which is the wonderful Byzantine church of Ayios Nikolaos Korthiou. It is of the inscribed cross type, with a dome and two columns, dating to the late 12th century. It is said that the chapel beside it was once a "secret school" during the period of Turkish rule. The district is clearly aristocratic. In fact, among the buildings in the region one can still see a feudal tower.

After Aipatia on the plain, we take the ascending road. As we approach Kaparia, we can see Ayia Marina and Alamania. At 7 km. we come to a right turnoff for the first settlement in Kaparia (phot. 3), which is Morakaii; farther along (8 km) is the main settlement called Vorina. Opposite is Pera or Megalo Horio (at 9.5 km, the righthand turnoff), where you can still see a group of very old buildings and farther along the little hamlet of Tzeo. There are many dovecotes in the region.

At 11 km, the highest point of this itinerary, we come to a left turn onto a road (4 km of gravel road) that leads to the monastery of Tromarchiani. A few metres later, another turnoff (left) leads to the Plaka site (phot. 2), with archaeological interest, and the picturesque deserted bays (3.9 km up to the Plaka Bay).

We are now on the western side of the island. The jewel of the area is the chapel of Ayios Georgios (Aï-Yiorgi) Farali (12.6 km), where one can quench one's thirst from the running water and enjoy the view.

Approaching **Zaganiari***, a typical picturesque little village, we can see a passable gravel road to the right heading to Kochilou (phot. 1) -Vouni and to the left at the beginning of a particularly tricky dirt road heading to the archaeological site of Zagora.*

At 14.2 km, we find the turnoff to the right leading to Zaganiari (the same road continues on to Alado). And the last building in the region is the chapel of Ayia Triada. Our trip is completed at 16.5 km, when we arrive at Stavropeda, the main hub of the region.

3

Two-day es

Andros is an island within easy reach of Athens and for this reason, it is certainly appropriate as a place to escape for a few days. Even better, it is the ideal choice for people who do not have the luxury of unlimited holidays and are restricted, in practice, to situations where they require an "oxygen break". So in addition to people who have the luxury of exploring the island metre by metre (see previous itineraries), Andros can also brighten up many monotonous weekends for those who may otherwise be stuck in front of the television set.
It is not our intention to scare you, but because we respect your need for rest and to get away from responsibilities and obligations, we are proposing a two-day excursion to Andros and have planned it so that you can combine rest and real recreation.

...ape to Andros

Arriving on Andros, at the port of Gavrio, the picturesque town that is the administrative centre, as well as an important trade centre for all of northwestern Andros, we invite you to become acquainted with it. It is the nucleus of a sparsely populated region, which is nevertheless extremely interesting from the point of natural beauty. Its main feature is its beaches. Either socially oriented or isolated, they are found north and south of Gavrio. The Fellos beach, on a delightful location, is worth noting in particular, just 5.5. km from Gavrio. It can be reached quickly and easily by road, despite which fact it has not yet lost its magic sense of the isolated and remote. South of Gavrio, in the village of (Ano) Ayios Petros, is one of the most impressive archaeological sites on the island, the famous cylindrical Hellenistic Tower of Ayios Petros, among the best preserved of its kind in the Cyclades. It is 5 km from Gavrio and offers a splendid view of the sea.

Our next stop is Batsi. The road, which runs parallel to the coastline, is in itself a sight worth seeing. Batsi is the tourist "capital" of Andros for reasons that are obvious. As we drive inland, we will go as far as the mountainous, lush but also solitary Arni.

Paleopoli is one of the most beautiful villages on Andros, one of the few spread out so impressively on a steep slope with such a dazzling view; it is sure to capture your imagination immediately. Paleopoli is also of special interest as it constitutes one of the most significant sites of archaeological excavations due to its classical past. In the local museum, open every Wednesday morning, the visitor can admire some of the finds that adorn the Archaeological Museum of Chora.

After leaving Paleopoli, we will soon be in Stavropeda, the island's major intersection. From here we can head to the Korthi region or abandon the west coast and head eastwards, to the densely populated Chora region.

A characteristic of this region is that most of its settlements, built on verdant slopes, are immediately visible to anyone driving along the regional road, while turnoffs on both sides lead to their centres. Among them, first in preference, is cool Menites, with abundant flowing water and examples of Andriot architecture in some of its more "noble" variations. Ano Menites and the entire route from there to Chora (i.e. through Strapouries, Mesathouri, Ipsilou) offers a view of this part of Andros that has been singularly blessed by nature, up to the eastern coast. At the end, it is worth taking advantage of two important opportunities before arriving in Chora. First of all, we can visit Apikia, with its famous Sariza spring and the important monastery of Ayios Nikolaos Neos (about 12 km from Chora), in a very pretty village, famed for the seamanship of its inhabitants. A popular beach here with crystal clear waters is Yialia.

This is followed by a visit to the capital called Chora or Andros. The neoclassical mansions at the entrance to the town, the Kairios Library, the stone-paved market and the Kairi Square with a plane tree generously

offering its shade, will alone make your two-day escape worthwhile.
The Archaeological Museum and Museum of Modern Art are nearby, and will satisfy
your artistic interest, as they host works by well-known artists from Greece and abroad.
The district of Plakoura with its elegant chapel of Ayia Thalassini, the strait
of Paraporti and the church of Theoskepasti, protectress of the island, Ayios Georgios Square
with the home of Theophilos Kairis and the Rivas mansion with the Maritime Museum,
the statue of the Unknown Sailor, the Venetian Castle
and the view of the Tourlitis lighthouse will move you
with their nobility and magnificence.

In Chora, you had the feeling of old-world nobility, and in the Korthi region you will undoubtedly delight in folk-style expression, which is mainly reflected in the vernacular architecture scattered throughout all the settlements. We would distinguish the Kochilou region. Built at the foot of a large limestone plateau, which for centuries offered a natural fortification to its important Byzantine and Venetian castle, it is a site suitable for observing the vast sea. A more modest but nonetheless charming view is that of the other settlements on the route, up to the coastal town of Ormos (or Yialos). This is where the financial activities of the inhabitants are concentrated. They have recently made great progress in terms of providing tourist infrastructure, in such a way as to show respect for the nature of the place.

Everywhere, good taste predominates. For swimming, the large beach is recommended, as well as the protected cove of Ayia Ekaterini. It should be noted that they are among the few "non isolated" beaches in the region. It is also worth taking in the relatively nearby

beach of the "Old lady's jump" (requiring a few minutes' drive on a gravel road and a short walk), a unique environment in a singular landscape. And finally, a visit would be of interest to Aidonia, one of the most representative of the leading villages of Korthi (1.5 km from Ormos). The aesthetics of the buildings, the remarkable ecclesiastical monuments and the most attractive fountain on the island demonstrate the superior taste of many of the region's inhabitants.

The entire route from Aidonia to Piso Meria (7.5 km on the sideroad) is a good alternative, if you want to head north toward Stavropeda. After leaving behind the last Korthian village, Kaparia, you could rest in the picturesque chapel of Ai-Giorgi Farali, and quench your thirst from the well, pausing in the shade of the plane tree to enjoy the view of the coves and capes of Plaka and Zagora.

As the weekend ends, we are certain that two things will have been imprinted on your mind: the unforgettable memories and the desire to repeat the venture!

INDEX

BIBLIOGRAPHY

Bistis, Leonidas, 'Ο ἀτμήρης ἐμπορικός στόλος τῆς Ἄνδρου ἀπό τῆς συστάσεώς του μέχρι τῆς λήξεως τοῦ Β' Παγκοσμίου Πολέμου (1882-1945)
(*The Andros commercial steamship fleet from its formation to the end of World War II* [1882-1945]), Athens 1982.

Charitonidou, Angeliki, *Andros*, Trans. David Hardy. "Melissa" Publishing House. 1981.

Damvergis Anastasios, *Χημική ἀνάλυσις τοῦ ἐν Ἄνδρω ἰαματικοῦ ὕδατος*
(*Chemical analysis of the Andros spring water*). Athens 1885.

Giannoulis, Odysseus, *Άνδρος: Συνοπτική ιστορία, λαογραφία, ταξιδιωτικές εντυπώσεις, μορφές της Άνδρου*
(*Andros: Brief history, folklore, travel impressions, and figures from Andros*), Empiriki, Athens 1964.

Goulandri, Dolly, *Περιστεριώνες στην Τήνο και την Άνδρο*
(*Dovecotes on Tinos and Andros*), Athens 1977.

Hopf, Karl, Η νῆσος Ἄνδρος καί αι εν αυτή δυνάσταί.
(*The island of Andros and its masters*). Andros 1885.

Kampanis, Petros, 'Η Ἀνδριακή ναυτιλία και ή ἐξέλιξις αὐτῆς ἀπό τοῦ 1883-1928
(*Andriot shipping and its evolution between 1883-1928*), Athens 1929.

Kampitoglou, Alexandros, *Ανασκαφές Ζαγοράς Άνδρου* (*Excavations at Zagora, Andros*), Archaeologiki Ephemeris, 1970, pp. 154-233.

- *Οδηγός των ευρημάτων από την ανασκαφή της γεωμετρικής πόλης στην Ζαγορά* (*Guide to finds from the excavation of the Geometric town at Zagora*), Archaeological Museum, Andros, Athens 1991.

Karagatsi, Marina, *Λίθινες εικόνες της Άνδρου* (*Stone icons of Andros*), Andros 1990.

Karapiperis, Leonidas, *Το κλίμα της Άνδρου* (*The Andros climate*), Athens 1964.
Kontoleon, Nikolaos, *'Ανασκαφαί Παλαιοπόλεως Ἄνδρου κατ' Αὔγουστον*
(*Excavations of Paleopoli on Andros in August*), 1956.

- Temporary exhibition of Publications of the Andriot Society, 1957.

Kyriakos, Dimitrios, *Άνδρος. Ιστορία και Πολιτισμός* (*Andros: History and Culture*), Athens 1965.

Loizos, Alexandros, *4 ημέρες στην Άνδρο* (*4 days on Andros*), Athens 1948.

Lygizos, Ioannis, *Παλιά αντριώτικα σπίτια* (*Old Andriot houses*), Athens 1983.
Megas, Georgios, Αἱ ἀγροτικαί οἰκήσεις τῆς Ἄνδρου
(*Rural habitations on Andros*), Athens 1948.

Mistardis, Gasparis, Τα ὄρη τῆς νήσου Ἄνδρου (*The mountains of the island of Andros*), Athens 1991.

Moschonisios, Nikolaos,
Η νῆσος Ἄνδρος ἀπό γεωλογική, ὀρυκτολογική καί μεταλλειολογικήν ἄποψην
(*The island of Andros in its geological, mineralogical and mining aspects*), Athens 1909.

National Technical University of Athens, *Οι Πύργοι της Άνδρου* (*The towers of Andros*), Athens 1983.

Paschalis, Dimitrios, Δημώδη τραγούδια τῆς νῆσου Ἄνδρου ἀπό τοῦ στόματος τοῦ λαοῦ συλλεγέντα (*Folk songs of the island of Andros collected from the mouths of the people*), Published by the "Dimitris Ballis" association for the development of Andros, Athens 1987.

- *Η Άνδρος κατά την επανάστασιν του 1821* (*Andros in the Revolution of 1821*), Athens 1930.

- *Οι χοροί της Άνδρου: Συρτος και μπάλος* (*The dances of Andros: Syrtos and Balos*), Transcription by Socrates Frangetis. Published by the "Dimitris Ballis" association for the development of Andros, Athens 1984.

- Δώδεκα ἐν Ἄνδρῳ βυζαντινά μοναστήρια (*Twelve Byzantine monasteries on Andros*), Athens 1932.

- Ἡ ἐν Ταυρείῳ τῆς Ἄνδρου μονή τοῦ Παντοκράτορος (The Monastery of Pantokrator on Andros), Athens 1932.

- Ἡ ἐν αποικίας τῆς Ἄνδρου γυναικεία μονή της Αγίας Μαρίνης (*The Convent of Ayia Marina on Andros*), Athens 1935.

- Ἡ Θεοσκέπαστη τῆς Ἄνδρου. *(The Theoskepasti of Andros*).
- *Η Άνδρος* (*Andros*). Publication of the Association of Andriots in New York, 1939.

- *Μονή της Αγίας Ειρήνης* (*Convent of Ayia Eirini*). Reprint from the Andriot Calendar, 1930.

Petrocheilou, Anna, Konstantinos Pantoulas, Theodoros Kitselis, *Το σπήλαιο της Άνδρου* (*The cave on Andros*), Andros 1994.

Polemis, Dimitrios, Ἐικόνες από τῆν Ἄνδρον τοῦ 1840*:* (*Images of Andros in 1840*): The Tower Illustrated Book, Andros 1987.

- *Οι αφεντότοποι της Άνδρου* (*The noble sites of Andros*), Andros 1995.

- *Ιστορία της Άνδρου* (*History of Andros*), Andros 1981.

- *Τα ιστιοφόρα της Άνδρου* (*The sailing ships of Andros*), Andros 1991

Polykandriotis, Dorotheos, *Το μοναστήρι της Παναχράντου στην Άνδρο* (The monastery of the Panachrantou on Andros), Andros 1995.

Televantou, Christina, *Ο γεωμετρικός οικισμός της Υψηλής* (*The Geometric settlement at Ipsili*), Andros 1993.

Verouki, Christina, *Κρήνες της Άνδρου* (Fountains of Andros). Andros 1991.
Vournas, Tassos, *Θεόφιλος Καϊρης* (*Theofilos Kairis*).